THE PAPER PLAYHOUSE

Awesome Art Projects for Kids
USING PAPER, BOXES, AND BOOKS

Katrina Rodabaugh

Quarry Books
100 Cummings Center, Suite 406L
Beverly, MA 01915
quarrybooks.com • www.craftside.net

First published in the United States of America in 2015 by
Quarry Books, a member of
Quarto Publishing Group USA Inc.
100 Cummings Center
Suite 406-L
Beverly, Massachusetts 01915-6101
Telephone: (978) 282-9590
Fax: (978) 283-2742
www.quarrybooks.com
Visit www.Craftside.net for a behind-the-scenes peek at our crafty world!

10 9 8 7 6 5 4 3 2 1

ISBN: 978-1-59253-980-2

Digital edition published in 2015
eISBN: 978-1-62788-341-2

Library of Congress Cataloging-in-Publication Data available

Cover and Book Design: Raquel Joya
Photography: Leslie Sophia Lindell
Gallery Images: By the artists, except where otherwise indicated.

Printed in China

For my son, Maxwell Forest—
my light, my moon.

CONTENTS

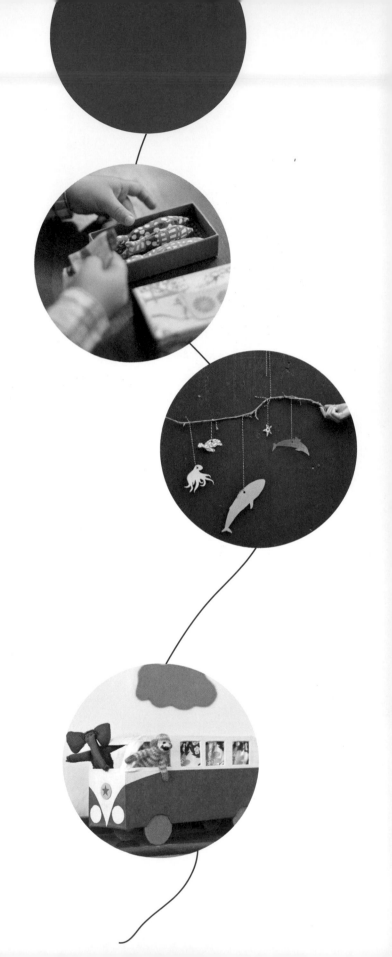

INTRODUCTION ::::::::::::::::::::

Welcome to *The Paper Playhouse*. I'd like to imagine this book contains all of the inspiration you would need to outfit a dream playhouse from top to bottom. Enter the playhouse doors, and you'll find handmade birdhouses, garlands, mobiles, monsters, notebooks, costumes, cars, dollhouses, paper airplanes, and even a lemonade stand. It's your imaginary studio for all things paper, just waiting to be transformed. This playhouse is your space to create, to imagine, and hopefully, to adore.

The list of potential art materials takes us no farther away than our own mailboxes, desk drawers, kitchen cupboards, and recycling bins. The possibilities for using and reusing found materials are endless. Even when we focus on materials made of paper—books, boxes, newspapers, magazines, maps, and decorative papers of all shades and textures—we are still flooded with potential. Now, add children to this mix of inspiration and the ideas multiply exponentially. Endless.

In creating this book I have three goals in mind: to foster inspiration, to make art accessible, and to encourage adults and children to see the creative potential in castoff materials. I want you to feel as if you have permission. I want you to feel as if you have full access. And I want you to feel inspired! These projects are not meant to be created perfectly without a wrinkle, dent, or other "imperfection." They are not meant to be replicated exactly or with great precision. Instead, they are meant to be used as a starting point. As an entryway into making art projects using paper, boxes, and books. They are meant to be enjoyed by children and adults alike.

Whether you make these projects alongside your little ones or intend to make them as gifts, I hope you will follow your own instincts for color, texture, shape, and materials. I hope you will view my instructions as guidelines and not rules. More simply, I hope you will make things. And, of course, I hope you will use this book to connect with the creativity of children through art.

Be inspired, collect materials, make plenty of mistakes, take breaks when you get tired, and sip that lemonade. And, ultimately, if you just aren't sure or if something is pulling you in a different direction than what I've created—please go ahead and make it up. Yes, make it up. Feel empowered to truly make these creations your own. The projects in this book are meant to encourage you, inspire you, and, ultimately, engage you with creativity. They are meant to fill your home with the possibility and power of art.

Welcome to *The Paper Playhouse*. Please, make yourself at home.

xoxo,

Katrina

GETTING STARTED

SOURCING AND REUSING MATERIALS, BASIC TOOLS, STAYING ORGANIZED, AND CARVING OUT CREATIVE SPACE

The majority of the projects in this book rely on recycled or upcycled materials. The hope is that you will start to view castoff objects as filled with potential for art and craft projects. You might need to save materials for a few weeks before you have all that you need for these projects, or you might want to ask friends, neighbors, grocery stores, or shipping centers if you can have their leftovers.

Boxes come in all shapes and sizes, and I encourage you to alter the project instructions to fit your materials. That said, there is a difference in the weight and construction of various boxes, so if the project calls for shipping boxes, know that any corrugated cardboard box would probably do just fine as long as it's an adequate size. If a project calls for shoeboxes it's likely that cereal boxes, cracker boxes, or tea boxes will be fine as long as they are big enough. As for the decorative/recycled paper materials you'll need throughout this book—be creative!

Build an arsenal of pretty recycled papers—birthday cards, security envelopes, maps, magazine covers, old calendars, small posters, business cards, and wrapping paper—ready to be upcycled into art projects. Nearly any favorite scrap can be fodder for future artwork. Even if there's just a small, 1" (2.5 cm) image that you really love—that's probably enough for a garland circle, the center of a rosette, or an added detail on a small book cover.

Once you turn your attention to the beautiful paper scraps available to you, you will quickly build a hefty stash. Again, you might need to build this stash before beginning these projects. Once I realized the potential in the patterns on the inside of security envelopes, they quickly found their way into my work. Now my husband automatically puts the most unique patterns on my desk once he's sorted the mail—they are just too good to pass up.

When using recycled paper materials, consider the overall condition—is it folded, dented, bent, warped, or otherwise damaged? If so, that doesn't necessarily mean it won't work. Can you use part of the paper and recycle the rest? Has the paper simply been rolled and not folded? If so, you can probably let it rest under weight and smooth out the curls, but you might not be able to smooth out folds. Search your recycled materials for evidence of glue, tape, and stickers, and remove these adhesives right away—even remove price tags from new paper immediately so that they do not leave a mark.

Water is paper's worst enemy, so if the found paper is wet, damp, or moldy, its best sorting place might be the recycling bin. That said, I have managed to wipe off very minor watermarks before they completely soaked into the paper. Simply use your best judgment.

The Paper Playhouse

If it's covered in mold, dust, or otherwise badly soiled, then it's best to pass on it and wait for more beautiful recycled materials that are likely just around the next bend. Once you get into the habit of looking at recycled items as potential art materials, you'll start noticing the creative possibilities in ordinary objects, such as paper, boxes, and books.

Whenever you're gluing two papers together, consider the paper grain. Don't go against the grain when adhering papers, because this tension will cause the papers to curl, warp, or separate. Determine the grain of the paper by gently curling the paper at the edge and lightly bouncing your hand on the curl—do not bounce so hard you create a fold. Then repeat on the opposite edge. The edge that gives most easily is the grain-long side. Determine the grain on the two papers and then join along the grain-long edges. This will help you determine how to position papers when cutting, because you'll cut according to the design and the grain. In this case, you do not want to go against the grain.

Also, throughout the book, glued papers will need to dry under the weight of heavy books. If there is any glue seeping from your papers, wipe it away and then sandwich the glued papers between wax paper or parchment paper to avoid damaging the books used as weights. Encyclopedias, phone books, or stacks of hardcover books work well to weight glued papers, encouraging them to dry flat.

The Paper Playhouse

BASIC TOOLS

When creating these projects, I tried to keep the required tools to a minimum. I also tried to create alternatives, such as using scissors instead of a craft knife, using double-sided tape instead of glue, or using ink instead of paint. Of course, you are welcome to alter the materials and techniques as you go along—make it up.

Many of the projects in this book can be made by kids, but most will require careful adult supervision. The projects were created assuming that adults and children would be working together. Of course I hope that adults might delight in making the projects for children, or to indulge their own sense of playfulness and kid-friendly design. Please use your own judgment when deciding whether to let kids use various tools, because you know their ability and familiarity better than anyone. Do err on the side of caution. When working with the children in this book, age was a less reliable means of assessing tool usage and technical abilities than the child's own experience and disposition.

You will definitely need some basic crafting tools, including various tapes, glues, rulers, scissors, pencils, craft knives, and ink or paint. If you think you'll make numerous paper projects, I suggest you invest in a few additional materials—a self-healing cutting mat and a metal ruler of the same length, a quality craft knife with extra blades, quality scissors in two sizes (strong for hefty cutting and precise for detailed cutting), a printmaker's brayer for rolling ink, and a bone folder for making beautiful creases. Your local art or craft supply store should have most of these items in stock but, if not, you should be able to find them online easily. Tools such as stamps, stamp pads, and paper punches tend to be used over and over for various projects, but you can build a stash of these decorative tools as you go.

STAYING ORGANIZED

The old adage that artists are disorganized is simply not true. People are either organized or disorganized and artists fall evenly across this spectrum. Whether you are organized or disorganized by nature, I highly encourage you to keep your tools, materials, and creative space as organized as possible. This will allow you to quickly assess your materials, more easily find your tools, and spend less time preparing.

For parents with small children, we know that time management and thoughtful organization are essential to a functioning household. Most parents have a handful of meals they can create with minimal ingredients, minimal time, and maximum satisfaction. Think of your art tools in the same way you think of

your kitchen—labeled spices, memorized recipes, and clean dishes are just a few of the things you take for granted. Go ahead and spend some time identifying tins, boxes, bins, and crates that can be used to house art materials, studio tools, and even recycled papers.

I suggest storing boxes and large sheets of paper flat under your bed; cutting scrap papers into more appealing rectangular or square shapes and fastening them with binder clips; and using canning jars, old tea tins, or large mugs to store scissors, pencils, pens, and paint brushes. The less time you spend locating your materials, the more time you can spend on the fun parts—making art with children.

CARVING OUT CREATIVE SPACE

I live in a 650-square-foot (198-square-meter) apartment with my husband and toddler. Like many city-dwellers, we work, study, play, sleep, eat, bathe, and dream in this beautiful, light-filled, albeit tiny living space. The biggest challenge? My husband and I work from home! Carving out creative space has never been more of a challenge. Nor has it ever been more important or rewarding, either. But we've done it, and you can, too.

Do you have an extra closet, forgotten corner, or unused dining room table that could be converted into creative space? What about that empty corner in your living room—is it big enough for a small table and two small chairs? Or maybe the entryway could double as your family art studio? What cuter way to welcome guests and enter your own home than through a well-loved art-filled home gallery. Trust me, if you want to find dedicated creative space, you just have to look around your home with determination.

Guest bedrooms, formal dining rooms, insulated porches, and finished basements are easily adapted into family art studios, but in even smaller spaces, a corner, closet, or otherwise-overlooked nook can be easily converted into a place for art-making. Once you have decided on the space, add a work surface, a chair, and a system for storage (shelves, drawers, stacked vintage suitcases, or crates, etc.) to keep materials organized and ready. Consider using a few feet of twine and some clothespins to create an inspiration board, encouraging all family members to pin up favorite postcards, paint chips, or poems. Inspiration boards can also be focused on a specific theme, such as inspiring a child's bedroom makeover, identifying the next family camping location, or just guiding your choices in making a project in this book.

Last, Ashlyn Gibson, one of the contributors to this book, is also the author of the gorgeous and inspiring interior decorating book, *The Creative Family Home*. I suggest using Ashlyn's book to guide you in creating kid-friendly spaces that are also rich with adult-friendly design. You can create family homes that are highly functional and highly fashionable. I promise.

CHAPTER 1: PAPER

JUNK MAIL, SECURITY ENVELOPES, FILE FOLDERS, MAGAZINES, GREETING CARDS, CALENDARS, AND DECORATIVE PAPERS

Our mailboxes, bookshelves, and recycling bins are virtually overflowing with the materials necessary to decorate bedrooms and playhouses, create moveable monsters, and evoke fuzzy bears from various continents. The insides of security envelopes easily transform into beautiful, modern, decorative papers that pair well with bits of greeting cards, calendars, or specialty papers from an art supply store.

Paper garlands are truly one of the easiest projects you can make. Like most of the projects in this book, they are intended for children but also meant to delight the imagination of adults. Although most of the projects in this section could be made entirely from reused or re-imagined materials, you are also welcome to mix old with new and indulge yourself or your children with a trip to the nearby art supply store.

PRETTY PAPER GARLANDS

Consider yourself forewarned: These paper garlands are addictive! What may seem like an innocent foray into using paper scraps can easily turn into a need for whimsical garland decoration at every turn. They look great hung in doorways, on the corners of framed photographs or artwork, looped over curtain rods, strewn over reading nooks, and even used as added decorations during holidays, at parties, or as a final flourish on a gift. They are so fun to make and to display. So remember, you've been warned. Now, proceed with happy abandon!

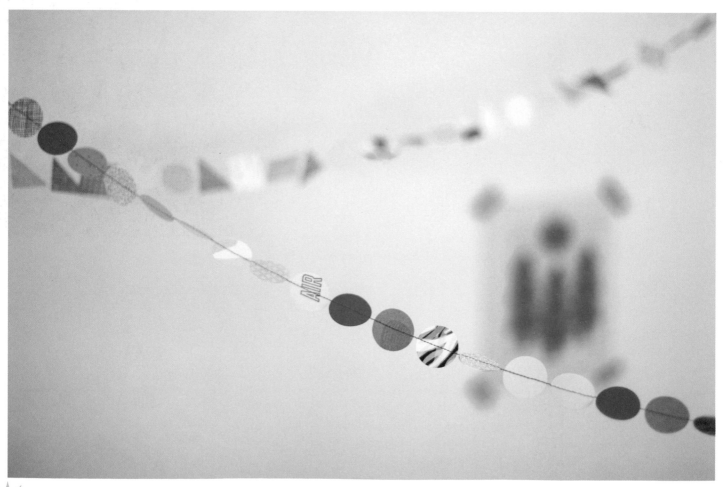

MATERIALS

* paper scraps—security envelopes, calendars, greeting cards, magazine covers, wrapping paper, maps, or any decorative or recycled papers
* paper punch, 1" (2.5 cm) or larger
* string
* scissors
* double-sided tape or glue

CONSIDERATIONS

Think about the color and patterns of your papers—how do they coordinate? If you're happy with your collection, then charge ahead. If not, consider adding or reducing the variations until you like your combination.

VARIATIONS

If you don't have a stash of recycled paper, dig through the recycling bin for magazines, newspapers, old wrapping paper, or other decorative papers. For future projects, begin saving security mail envelopes, greeting cards, or pretty paper packaging until you have a coveted collection.

INSTRUCTIONS

1 Prepare all papers. Open envelopes and remove any cellophane windows, glue, marks, dents, creases, etc. Consider including any unique design elements, such as handwriting, postage stamps, dates, etc. This is also a good opportunity to add children's drawings, paintings, or collages, which can be punched into small circles for the garland **(figs. A and B)**.

2 Lay the paper flat and punch with the paper punch. Continue punching papers until you have the desired number of circles. This project used 20 circles—10 on each side—to create a garland that measures approximately 30" (76 cm). Make the garland as long or short as you wish. If you are making a very long garland, choose a thread or string that is strong enough to support the weight of many paper circles **(figs. C and D)**.

3 Cut the thread to desired length and either tie a double knot at the ends or create a loop at each end. You choose how you'd like it to hang—draped over a nail so the tails dangle or hung around a nail so the tails are kept short in a loop.

4 Line up your paper circles in pairs in the order you'd like them to appear on the strand. The garland is double-sided, so arrange the patterned side of the circles in each pair to face out **(fig. E)**.

5 Lay out the length of string on a table.

6 Apply double-sided tape or glue to the "wrong" side of one circle in each pair and adhere the thread down the center before placing the second circle over the top, "wrong" side down. Continue assembling pairs of circles along the string until your garland reaches the desired length **(fig. F)**. Hang with irreverence!

RAINY DAY CLOUD MOBILE

The allure of round raindrops and oversized puffy clouds never really goes away. The promise of blue skies is just around the corner while the nostalgic pull of a rainy day spent around the kitchen table with crafts is just too strong to ignore. These paper mobiles can be made from magazine covers, book pages, maps, or any pretty decorative papers. Try using my favorite recycled paper—the inside of security envelopes—in combination with specialty papers from the art supply store. Choose your palette, coordinate your papers, find some pretty string, and before you know it, you'll have your very own cloud mobile.

MATERIALS

* Cloud Template, page 130
* Rain Drop Templates, page 130
* paper scraps—security envelopes, calendars, greeting cards, magazine covers, wrapping paper, maps, or any decorative or recycled papers
* paper punch
* thread, twine, yarn, or string
* pencil
* scissors
* double-sided tape or glue

CONSIDERATIONS

Choose double-sided paper for the cloud shape or use two different papers as a front and a back. Use a front and a back for the raindrops so you can sandwich the string in between. If you don't have double-sided tape, glue works just as well.

I GREW UP IN A CREATIVE HOME WHERE THERE WAS ALWAYS A PROJECT BEING MADE ON THE KITCHEN TABLE. BEING INVENTIVE WITH EVERYDAY MATERIALS OPENS UP A WORLD OF CREATIVITY THAT CAPTURES CHILDREN'S IMAGINATIONS. MAKE CRAFTING COLLABORATIVE AND RESIST THE TEMPTATION TO TAKE OVER. DON'T BE TOO PRECIOUS—INSTEAD TAKE A STEP BACK AND LET YOUR CHILDREN EXPRESS THEMSELVES THROUGH THEIR OWN CHOICES.

—Ashlyn Gibson, designer, stylist, author of *The Creative Family Home*

INSTRUCTIONS

1 Prepare all papers. Open envelopes and remove any cellophane windows, glue, marks, dents, creases, etc. Consider including any unique design elements, such as handwriting, postage stamps, dates, etc.

2 Use the templates in this book to trace raindrops and the cloud onto selected papers. Cut out two of each shape (front and back) for the raindrops. To make seven double-sided raindrops, trace six big raindrops and eight small raindrops **(figs. A and B)**.

3 Arrange your raindrops into a pleasing composition. Remember that the drops will spin when hung on the string. Consider staggering the raindrops or arranging by color **(fig. C)**.

4 Cut two strings into 30" (76 cm) lengths. Cut a third string at 12" (30.5 cm).

5 Arrange the raindrops in pairs according to size. Place the first raindrop in each pair patterned-side down. Apply a piece of double-sided tape or glue to the "wrong" side of this first drop, adhere the string through the center of the drop, then place second raindrop over the top with the patterned side up. You'll make this same sandwich for all seven raindrops, keeping the string in place and adding the paper raindrops as you go. When finished, you'll have two strings—one with three drops and one with four. The final drop on each strand will hold the end of the string **(fig. D)**.

6 Position your finished strings along the bottom of the cloud and use a pencil to mark their placement. Punch a hole into the cloud where marked. Punch another hole at the top center of the cloud from which to hang the mobile **(fig. E)**.

7 Tie each of the two strands of raindrops to one of the holes at the bottom of the cloud. Fold the 12" (30.5 cm) string in half to make a loop and attach to the top of the cloud with a double knot. Hang and daydream of sunny days ahead **(fig. F)**.

BEAR MASK MADNESS

When making a mask, the possibilities are truly endless—create a character, a celebrity, an imaginary creature, or a realistic animal friend. There's something adorable about children dressed as large animals. Maybe it's the play on size and scale, with tiny limbs and torso protruding from the face of a giant bear. These bear masks reach across continents, resembling the faces of our furry friends that roam the forests of North America and China.

MATERIALS

* Panda Template, page 131
* Black Bear Pieces Template, page 131
* cardstock or construction paper in black, brown, and white
* scissors
* pencil
* double-sided tape or glue
* masking tape
* chopsticks or straws
* file folder or cereal box
* craft knife (optional)

CONSIDERATIONS

Use any sturdy paper for the backing of the mask, but make sure no image or text shows through the white paper of the panda mask. A cereal box with the plain cardboard facing the white paper will be fine. Old manila file folders also work great—and provide a good excuse to purge your file cabinet!

INSTRUCTIONS

1 Trace the templates from this book onto corresponding paper. For the panda, trace the head on white paper, but trace the ears, nose, and eye patches on black paper. For the black bear, trace the head and nose on black paper, but trace the snout on brown paper. Leave the eye shapes until later **(fig. A)**.

2 Cut out all shapes **(fig. B)**.

3 Arrange the pieces for the ears, eyes, nose, and/or snout on the head as shown. Use double-sided tape to secure the pieces in place, taping the very bottoms of the ears behind the head, but all other pieces to the front of the mask **(fig. C)**.

4 Use a pencil to trace the eye shape to the mask. For the panda mask, trace the eye shapes directly onto the fixed black eye patches.

5 Cut out the eye shapes using the craft knife or scissors **(fig. D)**.

6 Trace final mask shape to a cereal box or file folder **(fig. E)**.

7 Draw a line ¼" (6 mm) inside the traced mask, creating a border all around it. Draw a line ¼" (6 mm) inside the eye shapes as well. This will keep the backing from showing around the edges **(fig. F)**.

8 Cut out backing along the lines you just drew, including eyeholes.

9 Line up the backing and the mask—if any backing shows around the edges, simply trim **(fig. G)**.

10 Secure the backing to the mask with double-sided tape.

11 Use masking tape to secure the chopstick or straw to the back of the mask. Use one long strip of tape vertically along the straw and two smaller pieces of tape horizontally to secure further. Enjoy your bear mask and practice your growl **(figs. H and I)**.

SCULPTURES FROM THE SEA

Mobiles combine sculpture and movement to create an object that shifts and changes as it sways in the slightest breeze, surprising and delighting everyone from infants to elders. There are as many designs for mobiles as you can imagine—hanging from one central point, hanging from several points, connecting to one flat object that hangs from the wall, or connecting to a round or square object that hangs from the ceiling. Each has its own special charm and invites movement and whimsy in its own way. This project uses a small tree branch or twig, which adds texture, shape, and line into the mobile's composition. It also allows us to forage in the yard, woods, or neighborhood park for just the right stick.

MATERIALS

- * Sea Creature Templates, page 132
- * twig
- * decorative and/or recycled papers
- * string
- * scissors
- * paper punch
- * pencil
- * double-sided tape or glue

CONSIDERATIONS

If you choose double-sided paper, you'll only make one version of each creature, but if you choose single-sided paper, you'll need to make a reverse image of each creature to make sure it has decorative paper on the front and back as you'll see both sides when the mobile spins.

VARIATIONS

The sea creatures in this project include a blue whale, dolphin, octopus, sea turtle, and starfish, but you could make any creatures you like. Choose a natural habitat such as the ocean, desert, mountains, or prairie and select five creatures from that region. Sketch the creatures until you're satisfied with their silhouettes and then proceed through the project with your customized plant or animal friends.

INSTRUCTIONS

1 Find the perfect stick! This might warrant a close look through the backyard, a trip to the nearby woods, or foraging around your neighborhood park. Of course, any size or shape stick will do, but it's an added adventure to search for the perfect stick—one that is so compelling you simply can't put it down.

2 Cut out the creature templates from this book or sketch your own. If you are using double-sided paper, simply trace the template once and cut it out. If you are using two pieces of single-sided paper, trace the template on the pattern side of one paper and on the "wrong" side of the other paper. Then you'll join the "wrong" sides to make the double-sided patterned creature **(figs. A and B)**.

3 Pair up matching single-sided creatures, and glue or tape, placing the wrong sides together. To ensure that the papers dry flat, place glued creatures under a heavy weight such as a thick book—dictionaries are great for this purpose. You might want to sandwich the creature between wax paper or parchment paper if you suspect the glue might leak out the sides. You could also glue papers first and cut shapes once the glue dries.

4 Make a tiny pencil mark where you'll punch a hole to hang your creature. Consider the weight of the creature when making the hole—you can test how the creature will hang by simply pinching the spot where you plan to make the hole and allowing the creature to hang freely. If it tips forward, move your hole up slightly; if it tips back, move the hole backward a bit. Once you're satisfied with the placement, punch one hole in each creature **(fig. C)**.

5 Arrange creatures underneath the stick. Adjust their order and heights until you have a pleasing composition, making sure your creatures won't bump into each other as they spin. Cut five pieces of string to match the lengths at which you've arranged the creatures **(fig. D)**.

6 Tie the creatures to the branch **(fig. E)**.

7 Test your branch in various locations, to find the perfect spot where all the objects hang straight. Adjust the location of the hanging string on the branch until you find the balanced position. Tie string to twig and hang from ceiling or wall. Put on your snorkel gear and enjoy! **(Fig. F.)**

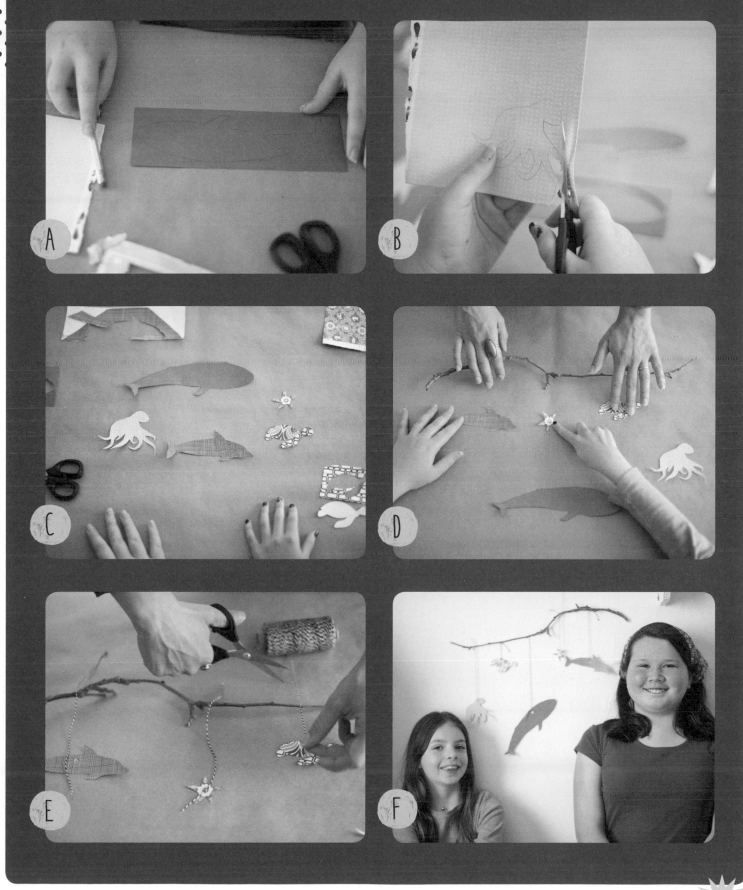

MOVEABLE PAPER MONSTERS

This project offers a modern twist on the classic paper doll. You can sketch out the sweetest or scariest monster and then add clothes, shoes, and accessories using your original monster as a template. You can even make an entire wardrobe for your moveable monster, complete with tiny wire hangers made from paperclips and a standing wardrobe dresser from a cereal box. This monster is intended to be on the sweet side—half bunny, half human, and 100 percent playful.

MATERIALS

* Monster Template, page 133
* Monster Clothing and Accessories Templates, page 133
* tea box, cereal box, or cracker box
* 8 small brads
* scissors
* pencil
* sketch paper
* decorative and/or recycled papers
* awl or hammer and nail to punch the original holes for brads, optional

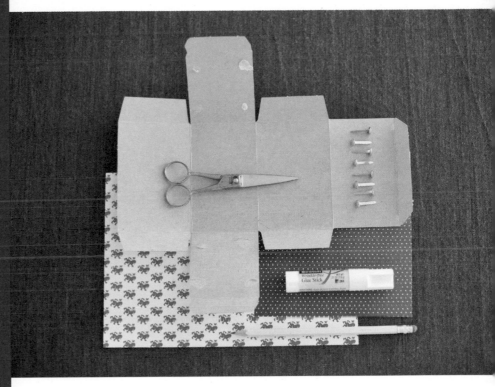

CONSIDERATIONS

Imagine how the clothes will interact with the monster and consider the brads, joints, and any other obstructions when designing the clothing. You might want to make clothes tabs larger than you think they need to be, as you can always trim if needed. Remember, some tabs might need to fold over brads or other obstructions so consider this when designing clothing.

INSTRUCTIONS

1 Use the Monster Template on page 133 to trace and cut out body parts. Or, draw your own monster on sketch paper. Revise until you're satisfied. Keep the shapes simple. Also remember that each limb needs to be a separate piece that will overlap at the elbow, shoulder, knee, and hip, making the limbs shorter when joined **(fig. A)**.

2 Cut the box at its seams until it lies flat, providing the most surface area for the monster's torso—limbs can be made from separate box pieces if necessary **(fig. B)**.

3 Cut out the drawn monster and trace its shape onto the box. Remember to draw each limb as a separate piece. You'll want one torso (with head), two forearms (with hands), two upper arms, two thighs, and two shins (with feet) when finished. Tip: Simply flip over the arm, thigh, and shin to make them mirror images of the right or left side **(fig. C)**.

4 Cut out all the pieces—you should have nine total pieces when finished **(fig. D)**.

5 Flip the monster torso facedown and use a pencil to mark where the limbs should attach to the torso. (Use an awl or hammer and nail if you need to make preliminary holes on the monster). Pierce holes for brads in each piece, making sure the holes line up where desired **(fig. E)**.

6 Connect the limbs by pressing brads through the holes and then opening the brads to fasten into place. Repeat for all the limbs until the monster is complete **(fig. F)**.

7 Use the Monster Clothing and Accessories Templates on page 133 to trace and cut out clothes or dress and accessorize your monster as you wish. Use the body parts as a template to make the clothes. Add tabs for traditional paper doll clothing that can be changed, or use double-sided tape to adhere the clothes to the monster. Dress your monster and begin your adventures! **(Fig. G.)**

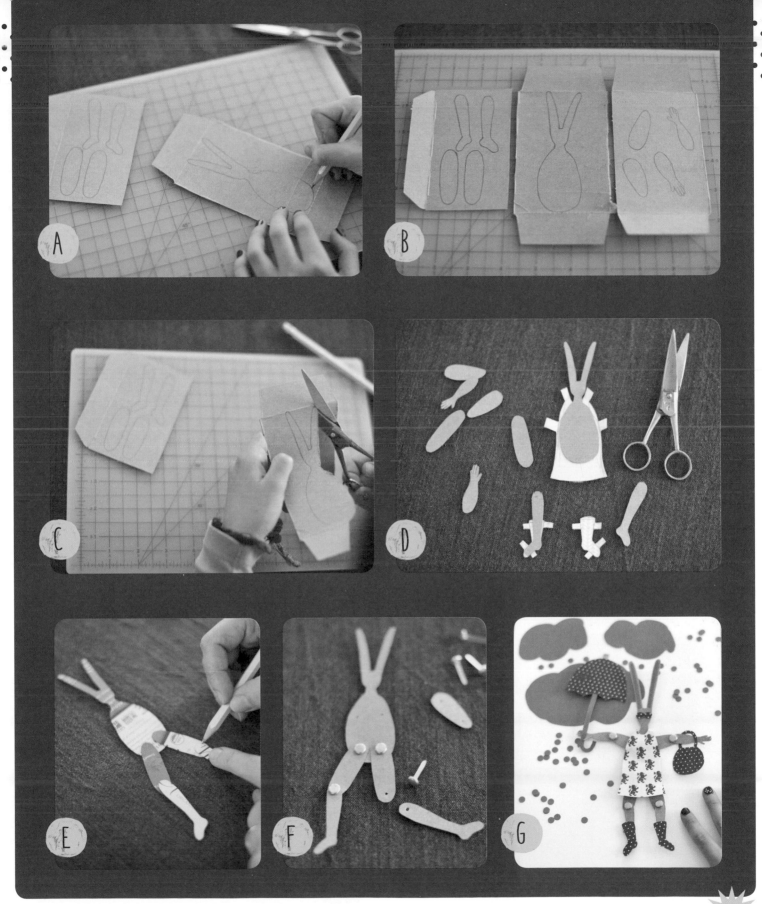

CHAPTER 2: BOOKS

USED BOOKS, VINTAGE BOOKS, LIBRARY CASTOFFS, NOTEBOOKS, AND OTHER BOOKS TO ALTER OR MAKE

There is something so satisfying about the weight, texture, and physicality of a hardcover book. Even beautiful magazines, newspapers, and maps continue to find their way into the contemporary design world, offering a tactile alternative in the digital age.

My own house is teeming with books—they fill one bookshelf and then demand another, they stack inside vintage wooden crates, and line the edges of my studio. I taught book arts to college students when I was in graduate school, and I was relieved to know that there was no shortage of bibliophiles in the next generation. Phew!

Book pages can act as the background for printmaking, collage, or beautiful paper art. Hardcover books can be transformed into boxes and pop-ups, and new simple handmade books and postcards can be created from various found papers and cardboard. We can even use the text in the book to create found poems or inspire mail art.

BOOK PAGE BLOCK PRINTING

Book pages are the perfect source material for various art projects. The text—and even images—adds rich layers to simple compositions and the words add another dimension to the final artwork. Sadly, too many outdated books end up in thrift stores, garage sales, and free boxes on city sidewalks—so think like a magpie! These pages can find a new life as original artwork, and their pretty aged patina lends itself perfectly to contrasting bold, bright ink for printmaking. Carefully tear out the pages, carve your blocks, and print your original images. Consider a series of unique prints: highlight specific words on the page with pencil, thread, or paint, or let the content of the book dictate your images. You could even cut away areas of the page to reveal paper behind, use collage, or paint over the page, masking most of the text. So many options!

MATERIALS

* Sun and Tree
  Templates, page 133
* book pages
* soft artist carving block
* brayer
* printing ink
* pencil
* sharp kitchen knife
* cutting board
* ruler
* printing surface—
  laping parchment
  paper to cardboard will
  work, too

CONSIDERATIONS

When designing your block, think about the content of your book page. If the book is about forests, consider making a tree block. Or if your book is about jewelry, carve a diamond. Also, when figuring out where to place your print on the page, consider any page titles, page numbers, and existing illustrations. You can use any carving block for this project but I'd suggest a block labeled "soft" or "easy to carve" because it will carve more easily than traditional linoleum or wood.

INSTRUCTIONS

1 Draw your shape onto the block with a pencil **(fig. A)**.

2 Using a sharp kitchen knife, cut your image away from the block. (The cutting should be done by an adult.) **(Fig. B.)**

3 Tear the book page from the book.

Tip: To get a straight edge, press a ruler firmly against the interior edge of the book page, where it presses into the spine. Pull the page firmly with your free hand. Continue to pull at a steady pace until the page has torn loose. Practice makes perfect—the more you practice pulling the pages against the ruler, the better your edge **(fig. C)**.

4 Ink your printing surface and use the brayer to roll out the ink until the consistency is tacky but smooth **(fig. D)**.

5 Roll your inked brayer across the top of your carved shape, taking care to cover the block completely to ensure that the ink will print consistently **(fig. E)**.

6 Flip your block on to the book page and press down firmly and evenly. To achieve consistent pressure on your block, use the palm of your hand, a printer's baren, or a jar lid **(fig. F)**.

7 Keep adding ink to your ink surface, rolling it smooth with the brayer, and re-inking your block as much as needed. When you're finished printing, rinse the ink off your brayer and your block so it's ready for future use. If using a glass printing surface, rinse the ink from your glass. Hang your new print and enjoy **(fig. G)**.

YOU'RE AWESOME ROSETTE AWARDS

There are so many moments in children's lives when we want to applaud their efforts and honor their achievements. Maybe it's the celebration of a major milestone, such as graduating from grade school and heading to the big-kid hallways of middle school, or maybe it's just an ordinary moment that deserves recognition such as a clean room, a finished book report, or losing a first tooth. Whatever the occasion, we want to celebrate our children nearly every day. So why not make the You're Awesome Rosette Award for every occasion? A wall of these awards would also make an artful display.

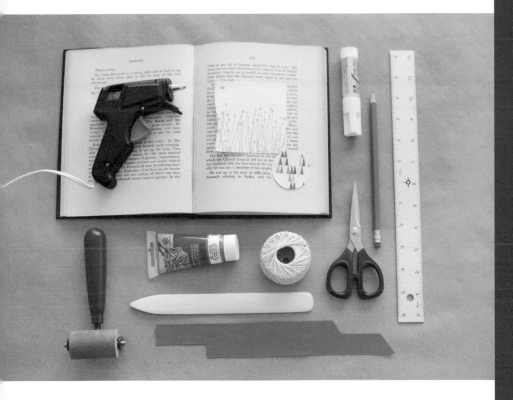

MATERIALS

* book pages
* ribbon
* decorative and/or recycled paper
* scissors
* ruler
* bone folder
* pencil
* glue stick
* hot glue gun
* hot glue sticks
* string
* printing ink or paint
* brayer
* inking surface—an old plate is an option
* paper punch, optional

VARIATIONS

Add various textures and color to your rosette by creating several concentric center circles from different papers. The award can be made with two ribbons instead of three, or it can be made with larger or smaller paper strips to vary the size of the rosette. Experiment! That's the fun part.

RECYCLING WITHDRAWN LIBRARY BOOKS IS A GREAT WAY TO TEACH KIDS ABOUT THE PARTS OF A BOOK. ALTHOUGH MOST LIBRARY AND BOOKSTORE BOOKS LOOK THE SAME, THERE'S A WIDE WORLD OF "ARTISTS' BOOKS" THAT CELEBRATE THE ART OF BOOKMAKING WITH HANDMADE PAPER, HAND PRINTED MATERIALS, HAND-SEWN SPINES, AND UNIQUE ILLUSTRATIONS. BY LEARNING TO PRINT, BIND, AND FOLD, KIDS CAN ENTER INTO THE MAGICAL WORLD OF BOOKMAKING.

—Jessica Smith, poet, editor, librarian

INSTRUCTIONS

1 Cut book pages into strips approximately 2½" by 7½" (6.5 cm x 19 cm). Make several strips—this project uses five strips per rosette, but the amount of strips will depend on their size **(fig. A)**.

2 Apply a dab of ink to your inking surface and roll flat with brayer. Keep rolling the brayer through the ink until you achieve a consistent texture that is simultaneously tacky and smooth—this is your optimal ink texture for printing.

3 Roll the brayer through the ink one more time. Then, using scrap paper behind the strips, roll the brayer along the edge of the strip so that it is only half inked. Don't worry about making perfect ink strips—the variation in inked widths will add charm and interest to your finished rosette. Allow the ink to dry. Repeat on the backside so the strips are inked on back and front **(fig. B)**.

4 Arrange the strips vertically on your workspace and accordion-fold them from bottom to top, using a bone folder to create crisp, clean folds **(fig. C)**.

5 Glue the strips together end-to-end, making one long continuous strip **(fig. D)**.

6 Pull together both ends of the strip to form a circle. Now, pinch the center of the circle together so that interior edges meet. Glue the ends of the strips together to secure **(fig. E)**.

7 Two people are required for this step—one person will hold the rosette shape along the outer edges and the other person will apply hot glue to the rosette center so that the interior edges touch. (See photo for detail.) Hold until the glue sets and dries completely. Glue the back side to make sure the rosette stays rigid. Hold until it sets **(fig. F)**.

8 Use a 1" (2.5 cm) paper punch to make a circle for your rosette center, or trace a circular object of similar size and cut it out. Using just a dab of hot glue, adhere the circle to the center of the rosette to cover all visible glue **(fig. G)**.

9 Cut three ribbons to about 6" (15 cm) in length. Glue to the back of the rosette. Add a small loop of string to the back of the rosette from which to hang it. Attach the ribbon and string with hot glue and allow to dry **(fig. H)**.

10 Trim your ribbon edges into double points and award your favorite little one for being so awesome! **(Fig. I.)**

FLY AWAY PAPER AIRPLANE

Paper airplanes are amazing creations. They can be made of most any foldable paper, the shape and design possibilities are endless, and the only true test of their function is that they actually fly. In creating this project, I researched several different paper airplane designs and settled on a hybrid made from standard printer paper or book pages using minimal folds that would hold up in any paper plane flying competition! Follow the photos to make this paper plane. That's right—put your reading skills aside and just follow the images for this project. If you make a mistake, start over. Or better yet, see how your mistake might actually improve the design. You are granted full permission to alter this airplane project as you see fit.

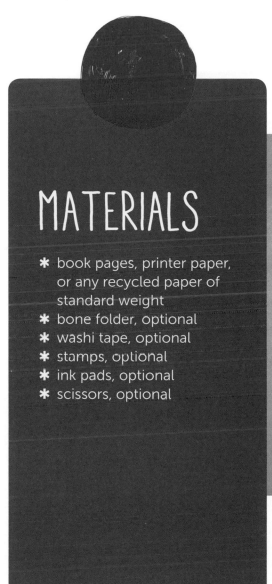

MATERIALS

* book pages, printer paper, or any recycled paper of standard weight
* bone folder, optional
* washi tape, optional
* stamps, optional
* ink pads, optional
* scissors, optional

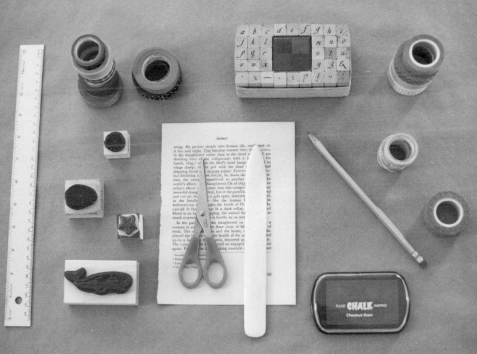

INSTRUCTIONS

1 Find paper—rummage through your recycling bin for printer paper or use castoff book pages for this project.

2 Choose any decorative materials, such as washi tape, stamps, or original pencil drawings.

3 Follow the folding pattern in the photos. You can do it! **(Figs. A–L.)**

4 Decorate your plane. Take these airplanes to the park or your backyard and fly away! **(Figs. M, N, and O.)**

MAIL ART POSTCARDS

Mail art has a long history among poets, writers, and artists. I once embarked on a thirty-day mail art collaboration with another artist and we sent each other one handmade postcard every day for a month. Not only was I running to check the mail by the middle of the month, the result was a compilation of my friend's mini original artworks—my own private collection. Choose a pen pal of any age in any location and agree to a handmade mail art project—maybe you just agree to one postcard a day for one entire week or maybe you agree to one package a week for a month. Or if a pen pal isn't in your interest, maybe you just want to pick a handful of people to receive your mini artwork via the postal service. It's up to you!

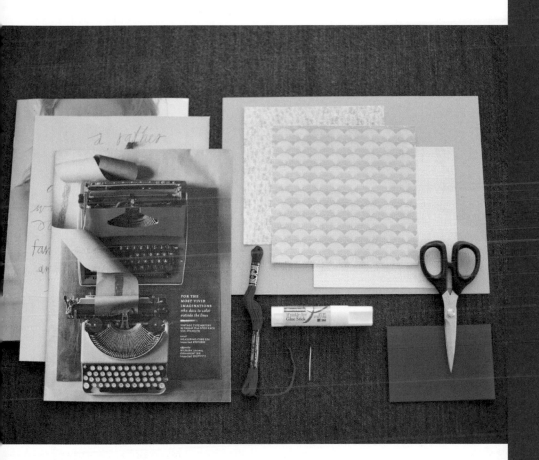

MATERIALS

* paper
* magazines, catalogs, or greeting cards
* cardstock or heavy patterned paper
* glue
* scissors
* needle and thread, optional

CONSIDERATIONS

Check with the postal service for regulations in size, shape, and weight of packages, envelopes, or postcards. We want to make certain your mail art arrives at its desired destination. Don't let the requirements scare you off—simply use them as inspiration.

INSTRUCTIONS

1 Choose paper or cardstock to use as your postcard backgrounds. Tip: If you'll be exchanging with a friend for a certain length of time, choose a theme for your postcards. Think of a character, object, location, or simply a color palette to build upon over the course of the exchange. Animals and balloons are featured in this project **(fig. A)**.

2 Cut background papers to 4" x 6" (10 cm x 15 cm) for this postcard project—feel free to determine your own dimensions, with guidance from the postal service **(fig. B)**.

3 Use glue or double-sided tape to add collage elements, stamps, drawings, stories, or poems to your postcard **(fig. C)**.

4 Stitch embellishments with thread and needle— it's best to use just the needle to create the tiny holes as your outline then go back through with thread to embroider **(fig. D)**.

5 Use mailing labels, stamps, or handwriting to write your message. It's easy enough to use a sticker or label to add writing where the thread shows through on the backside. Remember: Seal with a kiss. **(Figs. E and F.)**

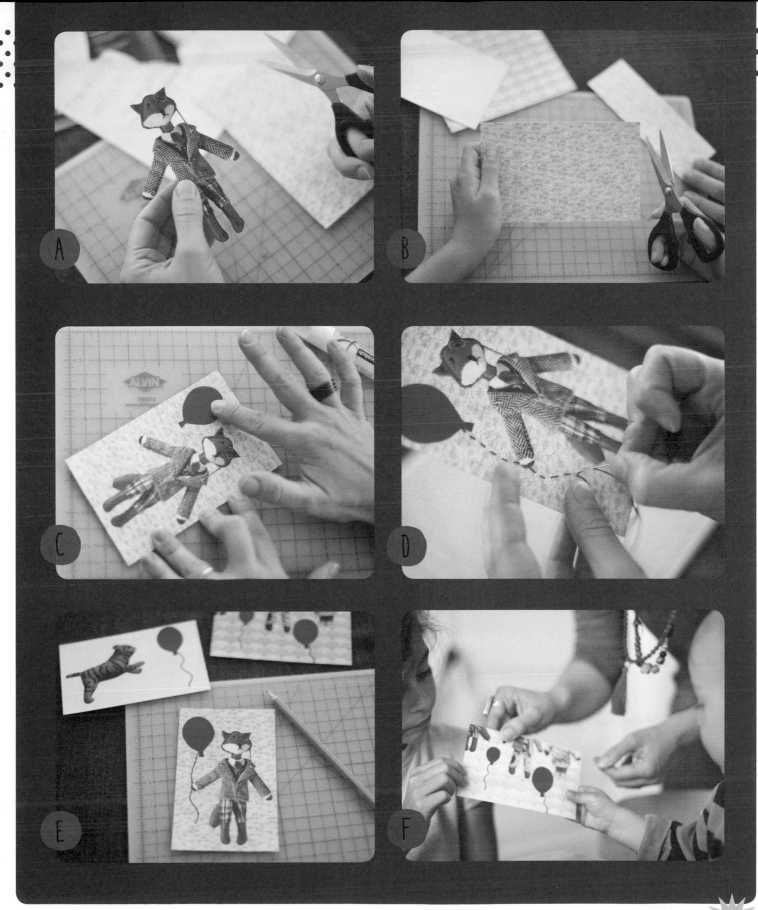

MAKE A MINI BOOK

There are so many variations on beautiful handmade books. Most bookbinders would agree that the three simplest binding techniques are the pamphlet stitch, stab binding, and accordion book. If you're interested in bookbinding, check out the artists Gracia Haby and Louise Jennison in the gallery section of this book, research bookbinding online, or seek out bookbinders in your local community. The world of handmade books is rich and inspiring. For this book, you'll use found papers to make a mini journal using a three-hole stitch. You can make the covers and interior pages as detailed or simple as you'd like.

MATERIALS

* heavier paper for the cover—magazine covers, catalog covers, or cardstock work great
* paper for interior pages—printing paper will work, too
* scissors
* bone folder (or a wooden ruler or wooden spoon)
* pencil
* ruler
* awl, optional
* needle and thread
* waxed thread, optional

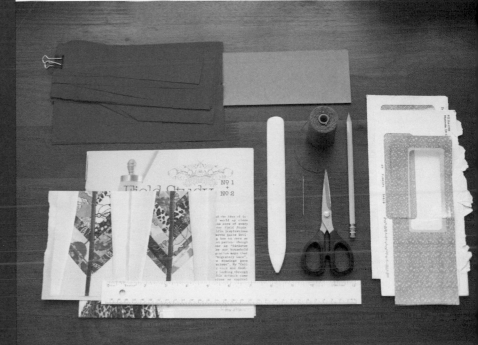

CONSIDERATIONS

There are often gorgeous covers on magazines, fabric catalogs, or even castoff books. Consider the size of your desired book when selecting the cover or let the cover dictate the size of the book—either way is fine as long as your cover and interior pages are similar in size.

I DIDN'T ACTUALLY HAVE THE COURAGE TO BE A WRITER UNTIL AFTER MY SON WAS BORN. SOMETHING ABOUT THAT INTENSE LOVE KNOCKING LOOSE THE FEAR OF MYSELF. BUT NOW RAISING HIM AROUND THIS LIFE OF POETS AND POETRY, IT MAKES ME SO HAPPY TO SEE HOW IT IS COMPLETELY NORMAL FOR HIM TO JOYFULLY WRITE STRANGE LITTLE STORIES AND MAKE BOOKS TO SHARE WITH FRIENDS. WE GET TO RE-SEE THE WORLD TOGETHER EVERY DAY AND CREATE A NEW WORLD ALONGSIDE IT.

—Samantha Giles, poet, director of Small Press Traffic

INSTRUCTIONS

1 Determine the length and height of your book. This project uses paper that is approximately 3" x 8½" (7.5 cm x 21.5 cm). Remember that you'll fold all papers in half, so this book will measure roughly 3" x 4¼" (7.5 cm x 11 cm) when bound. Use eight pages total, folded to make sixteen **(fig. A)**.

2 Cut all papers to size. You can make the cover about ½" (1.3 cm) longer and taller if you'd like. This will result in a cover that is slightly larger than the interior pages **(fig. B)**.

3 Fold the papers in half using a bone folder, ruler, or the edge of a wooden spoon. Start from the center of the fold and press toward one edge. Then start from the center and press toward the opposite edge, resulting in one complete fold **(fig. C)**.

4 Embellish any interior pages—Security envelopes make fun windows for collage. Just use a piece of paper roughly ½" (1.3 cm) longer and wider than your window as your background and add collage elements to show through the cellophane. You can cover the entire backside of the envelope if you'd like, hiding window and paper completely from behind **(fig. D)**.

5 Use a pencil and ruler to mark three holes on the inside of the centerfold of the center page—roughly at the center of the page and then ½" (1.3 cm) from top and bottom. Then use the needle to punch holes as marked. This should result in three holes along the fold from top to bottom (see photos for details). Make all the holes at the same measurement. If using an awl, you can carefully align all the pages and make all three holes through the entire pamphlet from center to cover **(fig. E)**.

6 Now that you have all three holes punched through all papers, you are ready to sew. Thread your needle but do not knot the end of the thread. Leave the thread tail at least 2" (5 cm) long. From the inside, guide the needle into the center hole **(fig. F)**.

7 Stitch from the center hole over the outside of the cover and then re-enter at the top hole. Pull thread taut **(fig. G)**.

8 Thread the needle through the bottom hole and back to the cover side. Pull the thread taut **(fig. H)**.

9 Enter final stitch by passing needle back through the center hole to the interior page. Pull the thread taut. Tie the thread end to the original thread tail and make a square knot. Clip ends to about ½" (1.3 cm). Find a private corner and begin compiling your first collection of poems, illustrations, or original collage **(fig. I)**.

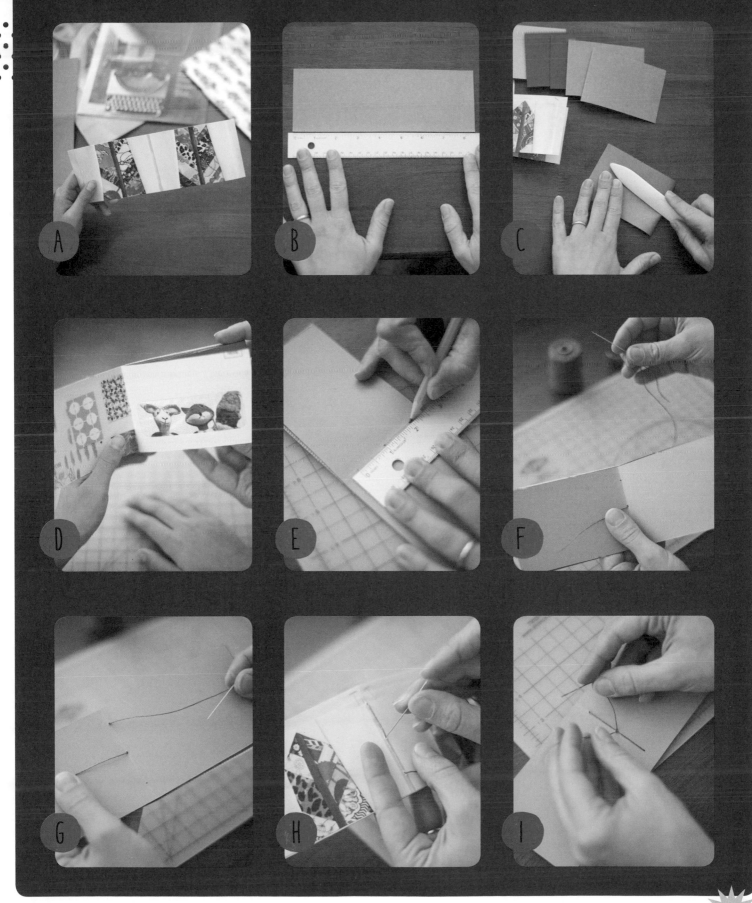

ACCORDION BOOK ADVENTURES

When I first learned how to make an accordion book a light bulb went off—I could make a book that looks like this! Liberated from the conventions of the traditionally side-bound book, I found the potential thrilling. It was the first step toward realizing that books could be art objects hinging somewhere between sculpture, design, and text. They could be filled with words, images, or only abstract markings. They could be made from paper or cloth, but they could also be made from metal, wood, clay, or any found materials. The accordion book allows us to create a simple structure that encourages a complex view of the wide and wonderful world of books.

MATERIALS

* 4 sheets of printer paper
* cereal box
* decorative and/or recycled papers
* scissors
* bone folder (or wooden spoon)
* pencil
* ruler
* glue stick
* PVA liquid glue
* glue brush
* cup
* magazine for gluing papers, optional

CONSIDERATIONS

Once you've mastered the accordion book, you can begin to work with more professional materials, such as book board instead of cereal boxes. Ask your local art supply store about their book board selection or do some research for an online source. Cereal boxes, cracker boxes, or even tea boxes will create beautiful covers, but be certain to align the grain of the box with the grain of your paper for a more professional book.

INSTRUCTIONS

1 Cut all printer paper to 9½" x 4¾" (24 cm x 12 cm) to replicate the featured project. If you want to alter the measurements for a larger or smaller book, please do! **(Fig. A.)**

2 Using a bone folder or wooden spoon, fold strips into four segments—three segments at 3" (7.5 cm) wide and one segment at ½" (1.3 cm) wide. (The smaller ½" [1.3 cm] segment will overlap the adjacent 3" [7.5 cm] segment.) **(Fig. B.)**

3 Glue all the strips into one long strip. The smaller ½" (1.3 cm) segment will overlap the next 3" (7.5 cm) segment so you will have one continuous strip of 3" (7.5 cm) segments. (See photos for details.) Place a sheet of wax paper underneath and on top of the glued areas and weight with heavy books until dry **(fig. C)**.

4 Cut the cereal box apart to lie flat. Determine the grain of the cereal box, as it's best to align the grain of the decorative paper with the grain of the box. (See "Getting Started" on page 10.) Using your ruler and scissors, measure and cut two 5" x 3¼" (12.5 cm x 8.5 cm) rectangles from the cereal box sides **(fig. D)**.

5 Find the grain of your paper, and align the paper grain with the cereal box grain before cutting. Measure and cut two decorative papers at 6" x 4¼" (15 cm x 11 cm), giving you a ½" (1.3 cm) border around the edge of your cereal box rectangle **(fig. E)**.

6 Place the paper print-side down and center the cereal box rectangle on top of it. Use a pencil to trace the shape of the cardboard box rectangle onto the paper and then use a ruler to mark each corner with a diagonal line as shown. Cut along these diagonal lines to remove the corners **(fig. F)**.

7 Dip the glue brush in the liquid glue and, starting at the center of the decorative paper, apply glue out toward the edges of the paper. Adhere the cereal box to the center of the decorative paper. Paying special attention to the corners, wrap the decorative paper border around the cereal box (See the Birdhouse Bungalow project on page 84 for details on wrapping board). Enclose the book cover in sheets of wax paper and place under a heavy book until dry.

8 When all the glue is completely dry, attach the covers to the ends of the folded printer paper. Glue the backside of the end segments to the inside of the covers to hide the unfinished cereal box and create the endpapers of the book **(fig. G)**.

9 Slip a sheet of wax paper between each of the just-glued covers and the first accordion fold and then place the entire book under weight to dry. When finished, begin your writing, drawing, or list-making adventures inside this handmade book **(fig. H)**.

SECTION 3: BOXES
SHOE BOXES, SHIPPING BOXES, CEREAL BOXES, MATCHBOXES, AND OTHER REUSABLE CONTAINERS

Our kitchens, offices, and closets are filled with potential art materials. Every cardboard box that comes into our home or workplace could be the beginning of a new creation. Boxes are easily transformed into automobiles, playhouses, dollhouses, cottages, and birdhouses, among other things.

I grew up in the country with a backyard that gave way to a field that gave way to the forest. Our barn, house, porch, and yard acted as temporary refuges to different orphaned animals—sparrows, bunnies, weasels, and our own baby chickens. I have fond memories of those tiny creatures gaining strength and staying cozy in various shoe boxes and other cardboard containers. I now live in a small urban apartment with my own growing family but find these temporary shelters just as useful. They are natural homes—and cottages and camper trailers—not just to country sparrows, but also beloved dolls, stuffed toys, orphaned flotsam and jetsam, and even imaginative toddlers and preschoolers.

Most of these projects rely on the help of an adult to use the box cutter or craft knife and to help position the cardboard pieces before securing with tape. They also rely on a child's imagination to fill these vessels with favorite toys, inspired décor, and endless adventures. These projects are meant to encourage three-dimensional play—thinking about space, shape, movement, and the sculptural possibilities of an ordinary box.

TINIEST TOY BEDS

Children have a fascination with the tiniest toys and objects. Perhaps sensing their own smaller space in an adult-sized world, they are simply drawn to tiny cars, stuffed animals, and even books that will fit inside their own tiny pockets. Something about the scale, size, or intimacy of a very small toy never seems to lose its appeal. Why not give those tiny toys the treatment they deserve with beds, sheets, pillows, blankets, and personalized spaces? Specialty soap boxes, larger matchboxes, or even empty candy tins can easily be transformed into tiny toy beds.

MATERIALS

* 1 found box to fit toy
* paper scraps
* small fabric scrap or felt scrap
* pencil
* ruler
* scissors
* double-sided tape
* stamp and stamp pad, optional
* pinking shears for fabric blanket, optional

CONSIDERATIONS

Look at the inside of your found container to make sure it's clean or can be cleaned easily. Usually a damp cloth will do the trick. If you don't have a paper box on hand, you could also wait for an empty candy tin or other small container. If your box does not perfectly fit your toy, that is completely okay; use this as an opportunity to get creative.

INSTRUCTIONS

1 Chances are that the child in your life has a small toy in need of an artful place to rest. Confirm that the chosen toy fits the box **(fig. A)**.

2 Measure the bottom of your box. Note that the inside bottom will be slightly smaller than the exterior bottom; simply measure the bottom and make adjustments later **(fig. B)**.

3 Using the above-mentioned measurement, cut one piece of decorative paper—this will be the bottom bed sheet **(fig. C)**.

4 To make the pillow, measure a piece of decorative paper that is approximately ¼" (6 mm) smaller than the width and ⅓ of the length of the box. Round the corners, if you like **(fig. D)**.

5 Cut the fabric at approximately the same width as the sheet, but to fit your toy—let the head of the toy extend from the blanket. The blanket will be roughly ⅔ the length of the sheet **(fig. E)**.

6 Using double-sided tape, secure the pillow to the sheet. Then tape the sheet to the interior box bottom **(fig. F)**.

7 Trim the blanket with pinking shears to reduce fraying. Edges can also be sewn, covered in felt, or you may hand stitch a binding.

8 Measure the outside of the box top, as you'll want to cover any brand names and personalize the bed for your toy. Stamps, stories, nametags, collage, or even decorative paper cut into simple shapes, such as stars, circles, or squares make cute coverings. Tape the decorations to the outside of the box **(fig. G)**.

9 Put your toy inside the box, cover with a blanket, close the lid, and watch your little one delight! **(Figs. H and I.)**

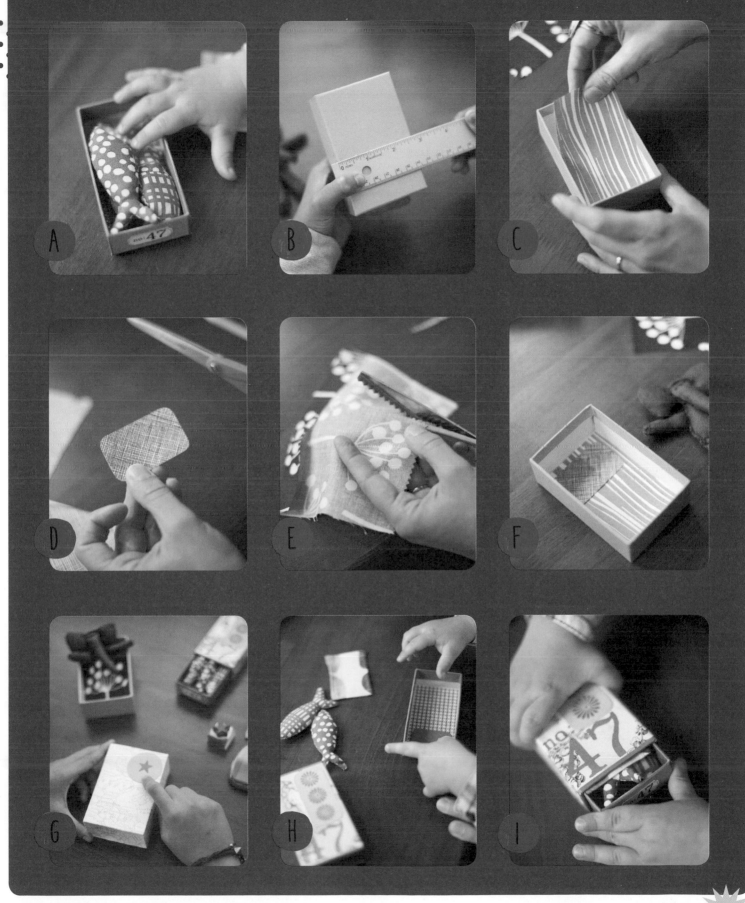

AIRSTREAM TRAVEL TRAILER

There is something so dreamy about a getaway on wheels. The promise of road trips, the romance of new horizons, and the portability of the comforts of home, all rolled up into one shiny package on wheels. The Airstream trailer also has a special vintage charm—the nostalgia of yesteryear combined with the potential for modern design. What's not to love? This project provides all of the above-mentioned benefits without the usual price tag or material investments. With cardboard, duct tape, straws, and some basic crafting supplies, a miniature Airstream can be yours in just a few hours. I'll leave the interior decorating and sense of adventure up to you.

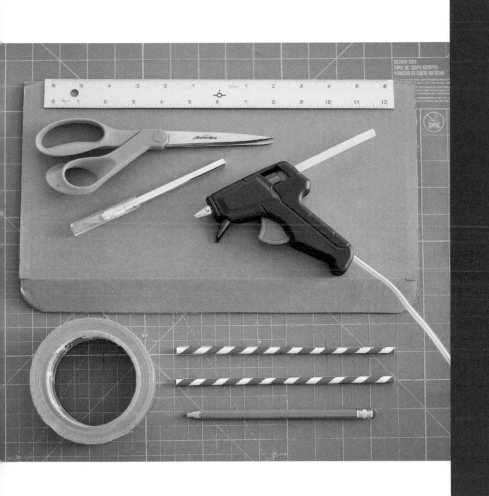

MATERIALS

* ***** Airstream Travel Trailer Templates, pages 134–135
* ***** shoe box
* ***** duct tape
* ***** straws
* ***** ruler
* ***** scissors
* ***** pencil
* ***** craft knife
* ***** hot glue gun
* ***** hot glue sticks

CONSIDERATIONS

Shoe boxes are typically the best weight for this project, as they are sturdy enough to create rigid walls, but flexible enough to conform to the rounded shape of the trailer and door. That said, a cereal box provides a lighter alternative, and a shipping box makes a more rugged structure.

INSTRUCTIONS

1 Open the shoe box and cut it to lay flat. Using the templates provided, cut the box into the three shapes—two big pieces measuring 6½" x 5" (16.5 cm x 12.5 cm) for the sides of the trailer and one or more smaller pieces that will be combined to make the long piece that forms the trailer back, top, and front.

2 Place the template on the big pieces of cardboard and trace to create the trailer sides. Cut out the sides and windows, but leave the door intact. If needed, tape smaller shoe box sides together to create a strip long enough for the back, top, and front (should be the length of the upper edge of the trailer side). Place the strip for the back, top, and front vertically on a workspace. Measure 1½" (4 cm) up from the bottom and 1½" (4 cm) down from the top. Use a ruler and craft knife to mark and cut out shape of windows as shown. Trace the door outline on the inside of the trailer side but do not cut through **(fig. A)**.

3 Cover all exterior sides with duct tape. Use a craft knife or scissors to cut out windows. It's easiest to cover the exterior sides completely with duct tape and then cut through the duct tape from the interior side so the window shape is visible while cutting. Repeat for the two large sides and continuous upper strip. Leave the wheels uncovered **(fig. B)**.

4 Cut the door on three sides only—be sure to leave the door intact along the interior long side to act as a hinge. You should now have all three pieces cut and covered, with windows cut out **(fig. C)**.

5 Tape the sides to the top strip. This is the hardest part of this project, so go slowly! Try cutting the tape in half to make thinner strips and use shorter strips to maneuver around corners. If the tape wrinkles, take a deep breath and keep trying! Gently bend the top strip to meet the curves on the camper sides—it's okay if the top strip cracks or bends. Remember, it does not need to be perfect, and wrinkles can add texture and charm **(fig. D)**.

6 Using the template provided, cut out two wheels from the leftover cardboard and leave them uncovered **(fig. E)**.

7 To attach the wheels, hot glue the upper outer-facing edge of the wheel and then attach from the inside of the trailer. The wheel will adhere best if attached to cardboard and not duct tape, so leave the space uncovered above the wheel cutout **(fig. F)**.

8 Make the trailer hitch using three straw parts. Cut two straw parts to the same length and one slightly shorter than the height of the wheels. Cover straws in duct tape **(fig. G)**.

9 Attach the ends of the two long straws to make a V shape, then tape the opposite ends to the front corners of the trailer. To make a stand for the hitch, tape the shorter straw underneath where the longer straws join. You might need two sets of hands to secure the last piece of straw. If the hitch feels unstable, line all joints with hot glue until it feels secure **(fig. H)**.

10 Add any additional embellishment or create a scene with toy cars and bottlebrush trees. Create imaginary campsites, secondary highways, faraway destinations, and your ideal vintage playlist as you begin your Airstream adventures **(fig. I)**.

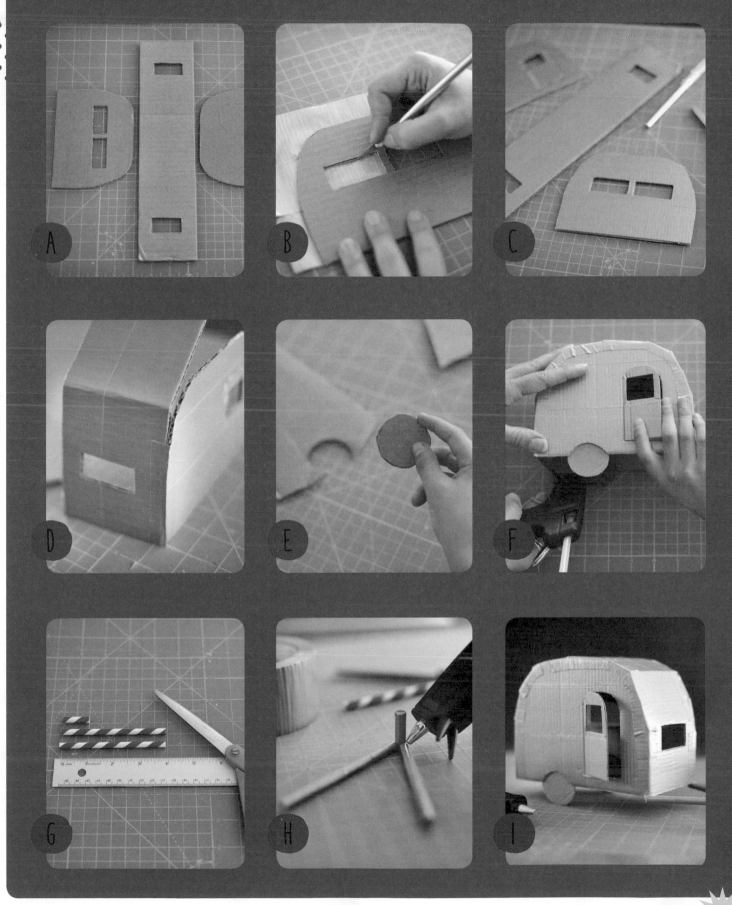

VOLKSWAGEN BUS BOX

The iconic Volkswagen camper bus conjures feelings of wanderlust, adventure, independence, and all the promises of a counterculture seeking peace, love, and understanding. It also begs for the addition of surfboards, mountain bikes, or enough kindling to make a campfire complete with marshmallows. It promises adventure. But if you aren't fortunate enough to have a VW bus in your garage, you can keep this miniature version on a desk, bookshelf, or nightstand so that dreamy adventure is always at arm's reach. Add a cardboard surfboard, a wire mountain bike, and a few cotton-ball marshmallows and dream away.

MATERIALS

* VW Bus Box Templates, pages 136–137
* shoe box
* two rolls of duct tape—white and blue
* fabric for curtains, optional
* scissors
* ruler
* pencil
* craft knife
* measuring tape
* hot glue gun
* hot glue stick
* pinking shears, optional

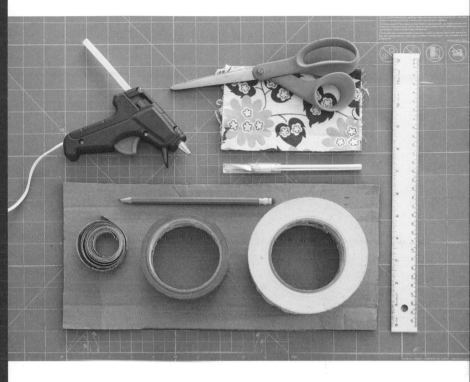

OPTIONAL

If you want to outfit your VW camper bus with curtains, you'll need approximately 18½" x 2" (47 cm x 5 cm) of fabric for six side windows and one back window. Each side window requires approximately 2½" x 2" (6.5 cm x 5 cm) of fabric and the back window requires approximately 3½" x 2" (9 cm x 5 cm), all gathered at the tops to make small pleats. Simply use pinking shears to trim edges and hot glue to secure the curtains to the interior top edge of the windows. Curtains, of course, are not required.

CONSIDERATIONS

VW camper buses are available in all colors, so choose the duct tape that best suits your tastes. I chose blue and white because it's a classic combination, but orange, yellow, red, or green would also be great combined with white for a two-tone finish.

WE'VE ADVENTURED IN VW BUSES OVER 20 YEARS BECAUSE HOME IS WHERE WE PARK IT. NOT KNOWING WHAT'S OVER THE HORIZON ALLOWS OUR ROAMER & SEEKER SOULS TO FILL UP. WHEN THE ROAD SAYS RIGHT, WE SAY, GO LEFT! EXCITING TRAVELS IN OUR VW HAVE SPARKED NUMEROUS ARTWORKS, DISCUSSIONS, & THE FREEDOM TO CLEAR THE HEAD.

—Jen Lake, VW adventurer, artist, maker

INSTRUCTIONS

1 Open the shoe box and cut it to lay flat. Cut it into three shapes: two large pieces for the camper sides and one or more smaller pieces that will be combined to make the camper back, top, and front.

2 Lay your template for the sides of the camper on the large shoe box pieces. Trace and cut out the camper sides, including the windows **(figs. A and B)**.

3 If needed, tape smaller shoe box sides together to create a strip long enough for the back, top, and front (see the template, it should be the length of the upper edge of the camper side). Cut out the shape of the windows in the camper strip to match the photo **(fig. C)**.

4 Draw a line approximately ½" (1.3 cm) below the windows and continue the line across all four sides. This line marks the two-tone paint finish—below the line will be blue and above the line will be white. Extend the white line into a V shape along the front edges of the camper and continue along the front panel until meeting in a deep V at the location of the front bumper. You can either cover the camper in duct tape now or after you've assembled, it's up to you **(fig. D)**.

5 Use duct tape to cover all of the exterior sides of the camper van. Use a craft knife or scissors to cut out windows. It's easiest to completely cover the van with duct tape on the exterior sides and then cut through the duct tape from the interior side so the window shape is visible while cutting **(fig. E)**.

6 Tape the sides to the top strip. This is the hardest part of this project, so go slowly! Try cutting the tape in half to make thinner strips and use shorter strips to maneuver around corners. If the tape wrinkles, take a deep breath and keep trying! Gently bend the top strip to meet the curves on the camper sides—it's okay if the top strip cracks or bends. Remember, it does not need to be perfect and wrinkles can add texture and homemade charm **(fig. F)**.

Tip: It will be easier for two people to attach the sides to the top strip—this is a great chance for kids and adults to work together.

7 Using a round object measuring approximately 1½" (4 cm) in diameter trace and cut four wheels of the same size. Alternately, use the template on page 137 **(fig. G)**.

8 To attach the wheels, line the upper outer-facing edge of the wheel with hot glue and then attach from inside the camper van **(fig. H)**.

9 Add details such as headlights, taillights, a front logo, bumpers, door handles, or hubcaps. Decorate with small toys that fit inside camper windows and proceed to the nearest imaginary beach, mountains, or desert wilderness where your adventure awaits **(fig. I)**.

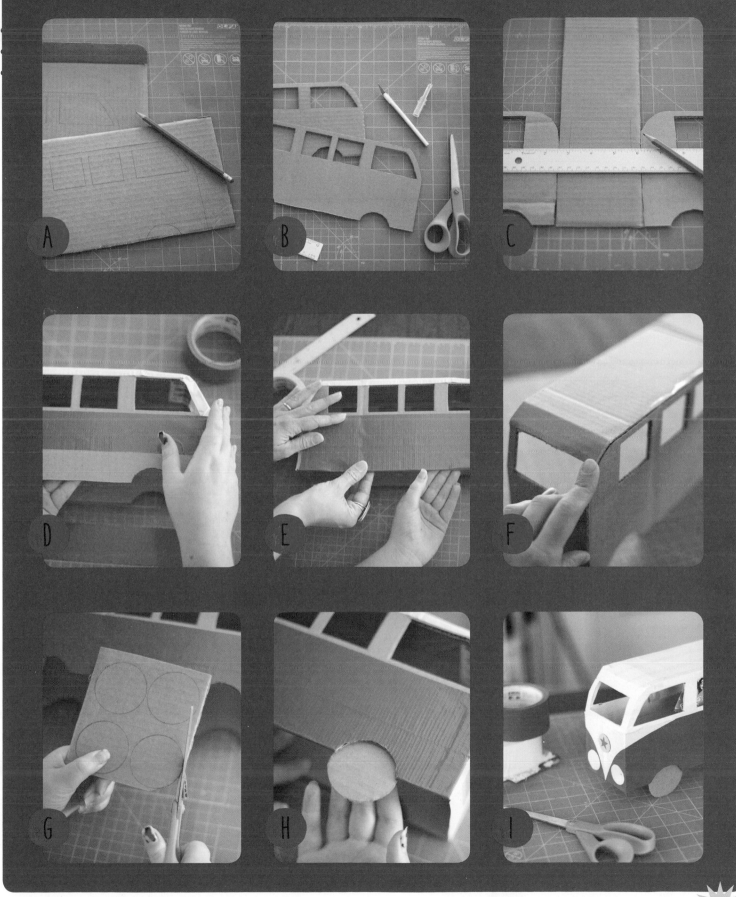

COTTAGE OR CABIN PLAYHOUSE

Many of us long for a vacation home—a place to get away from our daily lives and pursue leisure. For some people, this second home might be a contemporary condominium in a major metropolitan area, but for most of us, the idea of a vacation home conjures up simple cabins, quaint cottages, or otherwise cozy getaways. This project uses simple materials to make a cottage or cabin playhouse for the littlest ones. Although the shipping box will likely lend itself to the size of a toddler, this project could also be expanded to accommodate an older child in search of a private clubhouse.

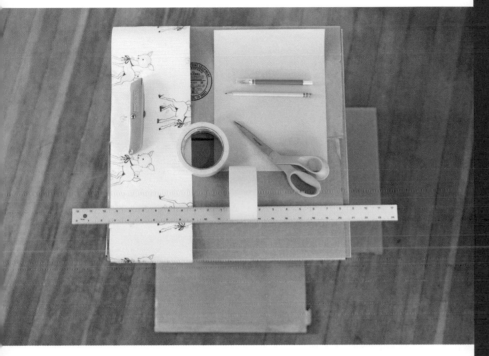

* 1 large shipping box
* decorative, recycled, or wrapping paper
* box cutter
* craft knife
* ruler
* scissors
* duct tape

For sign, optional
* computer
* printer
* print paper
* cup hooks
* paper punch

CONSIDERATIONS

The amount of paper and duct tape will depend on the size of your box. For this project, I used an extra-large shipping box, four sheets of decorative wrapping paper, and two rolls of duct tape. Tape the roof on one side only and the project will fold up for storage. Just assemble and add a strip of duct tape to the second side for play, and remove that strip for storage.

VARIATIONS

You can alter any large shipping box to make this project, but square boxes require fewer measurements than rectangular ones. Rectangular boxes make for adorable (and taller) playhouses, too.

INSTRUCTIONS

1 Cut off all top flaps. Cut off one entire side flap including the attached bottom flap, then cut off the opposite bottom flap. You should now have a flat box with three attached sides and two attached opposite bottom flaps. One side with attached flap will become the roof and two small bottom flaps will become the doors **(fig. A)**.

2 If you are using a square box, skip to step three. If you are using a rectangular box, trim the loose side flap (not the attached bottom flap) to the width of the two combined bottom flaps. For example, if your bottom flaps measure 8" (20.5 cm), then cut your loose side flap to a width of 16" (40.5 cm). This piece will become the roof so it needs to be the same width as the floor **(fig. B)**.

3 Stand your box upright, position the two bottom flaps to make the floor, and check to see that when you attach your roof it will look like the model. If it will, proceed to step four. If it won't, check your measurements and try again **(fig. C)**.

4 Cover the entire outside of the house, including the main box, the roof, and the two front doors, in paper and tape down **(fig. D)**.

5 Secure all exposed edges with duct tape, allowing the tape to wrap around the edges. When it is finished, the interior will remain uncovered, while the entire exterior (including the roof and two bottom flaps for doors) and edges will be covered in tape **(fig. E)**.

6 Tape the roof to the coordinating sides (or to one side if you want the box to remain foldable). This is a good time to stand the box upright and double-check the placement of the roof and then lay it down flat to secure with tape **(fig. F)**.

Tip: When taping the door, leave about ¼" (6 mm) space between the two pieces of cardboard to create a moveable hinge. If you tape the two pieces directly next to one another they will remain rigid, but if you leave a small amount of space between the pieces (covered only in tape) your hinge will move more freely. This is most important for the front doors **(fig. G)**.

7 Decide on your house details. If you want to cut windows, wait until you've taped the paper to the cardboard, then cut through all the layers at once. Tape all edges. It's easiest to add shingles, shutters, wreaths, or signs when the house is flattened, so remember to leave one side of the roof loose.

8 Personalize your house by making a sign for the front door. Make your sign by hand or on a computer—print, cut, and decorate. For the project shown, we used a paper punch to make two holes in the sign, screwed small cup hooks into the front door, and added the sign. Note: If you're concerned about a toddler putting the cup hooks into his or her mouth, tape the sign directly to the door **(fig. H)**.

Tip: Screw the cup hooks into the cardboard until you feel the pressure on the other side, but no more. Don't let the screw poke through. If it does poke through, no worries. Simply cover the exposed screw with a piece of duct tape **(fig. I)**.

9 Stand the house upright. For added support, tape the floor panels together and tape the final side of the roof to the wall. Add books, toys, blankets, pillows, and enjoy this tot-sized hideaway **(fig. J)**.

DREAMY MODERN DOLLHOUSE

There are as many designs for a dollhouse as there are blueprints for a family home. Fortunately, a dollhouse doesn't require heating, cooling, plumbing, or water systems, but give some thought to the shape of the house, peak of the roof, overall square footage, and number of bedrooms. Once the structure is complete, the fun begins! Consider wallpaper, flooring, furniture, artwork, textiles, and lighting. You could spend several weeks making this dollhouse or only a few days creating with the materials you have on hand. Regardless of your design aesthetic or paper choices, remember to surprise the little one in your life with personalized details—favorite animals for the wallpaper, favorite colors for the bedding, or a miniature version of his or her favorite toy as a resident.

MATERIALS

- ✳ 2 shipping boxes
- ✳ decorative and/or recycled papers
- ✳ dollhouse furniture
- ✳ scissors
- ✳ utility knife
- ✳ ruler
- ✳ craft paper tape or duct tape
- ✳ double-sided tape and/or glue stick

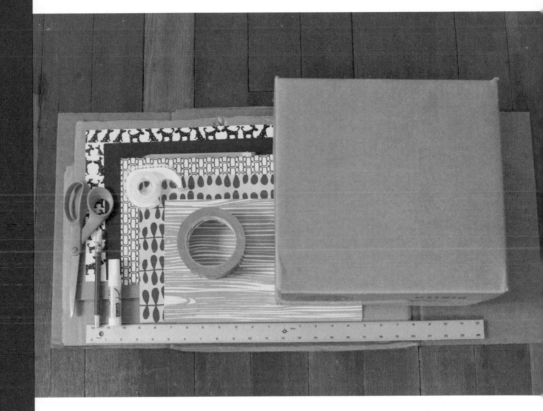

OPTIONAL

Invite children to decorate the papers used for the wallpaper, flooring, siding, and/or roof. Design furniture from upcycled materials—a cork with a rosemary sprig becomes a tree, a bottle cap becomes a cool industrial lighting fixture, and a scrap of fabric becomes a blanket or curtain.

CONSIDERATIONS

Use cardboard boxes of any size for this project, but make sure all sides are the same depth—if your roof sides are wider than your first floor walls, just trim to the same width. Use small shoe boxes to make a tiny dollhouse or large shipping boxes for a much larger version.

INSTRUCTIONS

1 Cut all the top and bottom flaps from box 1, but leave the sides intact **(fig. A)**.

2 Measure the height and width of box 1. Use the measurements to make the house shape (back walls) on box 2. The height of box 1 will determine the placement of the first floor, and the width will determine house width, etc. Tip box 1 on its side and draw a traditional house profile on box 2, including a rectangle on the bottom and a triangle on the top for the peak. Cut out the house outline on box 2 **(fig. B)**.

3 Cut out one additional piece of cardboard for the interior wall, matching the height to that of the walls in box 1 and the depth to that of the exterior walls **(fig. C)**.

4 Cut out two additional sections for the roof, making them the same depth as the exterior walls on box 1. The length will be determined by the pitch of the roof. When finished cutting, you should have five pieces—one box for downstairs, one loose interior wall, one house-shaped panel for back walls, and two pieces for the roof. **(Fig. D.)**

5 Tape all front-facing edges with paper tape or duct tape—this includes box 1, the interior wall, and the roof pieces. Tape the interior wall into place **(fig. E)**.

6 Decorate all interior walls, floors, and upstairs ceiling panels. You can cover the walls with plain paper and then paint or stencil them, or you can line the walls with decorative papers. Use a glue stick or double-sided tape to secure. Consider patterns, color, scale, flooring, furniture, etc. Cut out paper to cover exterior walls. You can even use paper to make shingles for the roof (see Birdhouse Bungalow project on page 86 for shingle instructions). **(Fig. F.)**

7 Attach the back house shape to box 1 with craft paper tape or duct tape **(fig. G)**.

8 Tape two roof panels together at the top leaving an approximately ¼" (6 mm) "hinge" between panels—this allows for easier movement in placing roof panels at the peak. Then attach the roof to the top edges of the back wall. If the lower edge of your roof meets the upper edge of your downstairs (box 1) walls, you can attach at the seam. If you have created eaves that overhang, you might need to reinforce with tape from underneath the eaves. Try cutting paper tape at desired width and then folding in half lengthwise to insert under eave **(fig. H)**.

9 Cover the exterior walls with decorative papers. Cover the roof with shingles if desired **(fig. I)**.

10 Add any additional details, including exterior windows, doors, flower boxes, etc. Personalize interior by adding miniature family photos, tiny beloved artwork, or get ambitious and weave miniscule throw rugs and blankets. No design element is too tiny! **(Fig. J.)**

BIRDHOUSE BUNGALOW

I have such fond memories of watching my mother tend to her various birdhouses, birdbaths, and flower gardens. She knew the names of all the regional songbirds and wildflowers and our yard was a virtual haven to her favorite feathered and floral friends. Living in urban centers for most of my adult life, I don't have the same relationship with birdhouses in my backyard, but I do still have the opportunity to observe local flora and fauna and sharpen my attention to the neighborhood songbirds. Although this birdhouse is intended for indoor spaces and inanimate birds, it creates a sense of whimsy and wonder for the great outdoors and for the promise of imaginary feathered guests.

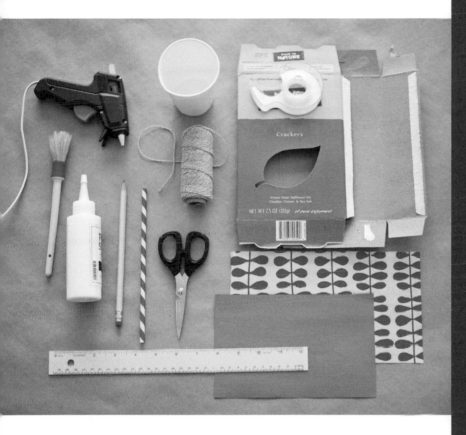

MATERIALS

* Birdhouse Bungalow Templates, pages 138–139
* cracker boxes and/or cereal boxes
* double-sided tape
* masking tape
* decorative and/or recycled papers
* fabric trim for the roof, optional
* straw (pretty paper straws preferred)
* thread
* ruler
* scissors
* pencil
* liquid glue (PVA preferred)
* glue brush
* hot glue gun
* hot glue stick
* cup to hold liquid glue
* old magazine to use for gluing

CONSIDERATIONS

Think about the colors, patterns, and textures you select for the birdhouse walls, roofing, straw for perch, and any decorative trim. Although the fabric trim is optional, it will help to hide any visible glue patches around your roof, so consider the color of your fabric trim in relationship to the areas it will mask—I chose red trim because it would conceal glue against the red and beige paper. These choices will help to create an overall cohesive palette while concealing crooked edges and puddles of glue. Function and fashion at its best!

INSTRUCTIONS

1 Open the cereal boxes flat. You'll need seven pieces when finished. Depending on the size of your box, you might need several boxes to make space for all seven sides.

2 Trace the templates and cut all pieces from the cereal boxes **(fig. A)**.

3 Trace all the sides (and bottom if you prefer) to the wrong side of your decorative paper. Leave the roof separate—these panels will be covered in shingles. Add ½" (1.3 cm) on all sides of your traced shape, creating a ½" (1.3 cm) border on your house sides. Cut out the larger shape, leaving the traced shape visible **(fig. B)**.

4 Cut all corners on the diagonal at 45-degree angles to the sides. Leave about ⅛" (3 mm) between the cut corner and the original traced shape—you can use the edge of a metal ruler to create this width and make the straight edge for cutting **(fig. C)**.

5 Using your glue and glue brush start in the center of the decorative paper and brush glue toward the outer edges **(fig. D)**.

6 Center the cereal box into place on the glued paper and press to adhere. Brush the border with glue, starting at the cereal box and moving toward the edges. Press the border over the backside of the cereal box—your mitered corners should fold into place when pressed. Repeat on all sides, then place under a book weight until dry. (Dictionaries work great for book weight—sandwich wet pieces in wax paper or parchment paper to catch any seeping glue.) **(Figs. E and F.)**

7 To prepare the roof strips, cut 1" (2.5 cm) strips of paper to the width of the roof panels. The strips will be layered to make shingles so you'll need approximately two strips per 1" (2.5 cm) of height—the strips will overlap so just the fringe is visible. Cut fringe at random widths and at ½" (1.3 cm) height. **(Fig. G.)**

8 Using double-sided tape, adhere the shingles to the roof by overlapping the strips so only the fringe is visible **(fig. H)**.

9 Using a glue gun, glue all sides to the birdhouse bottom. This will be easier with two people! You might also want to create a square guide to ensure that all sides attach at a right angle—two books set at right angles can also act as your guide. Hold each side in place until the glue dries and sets **(fig. I)**.

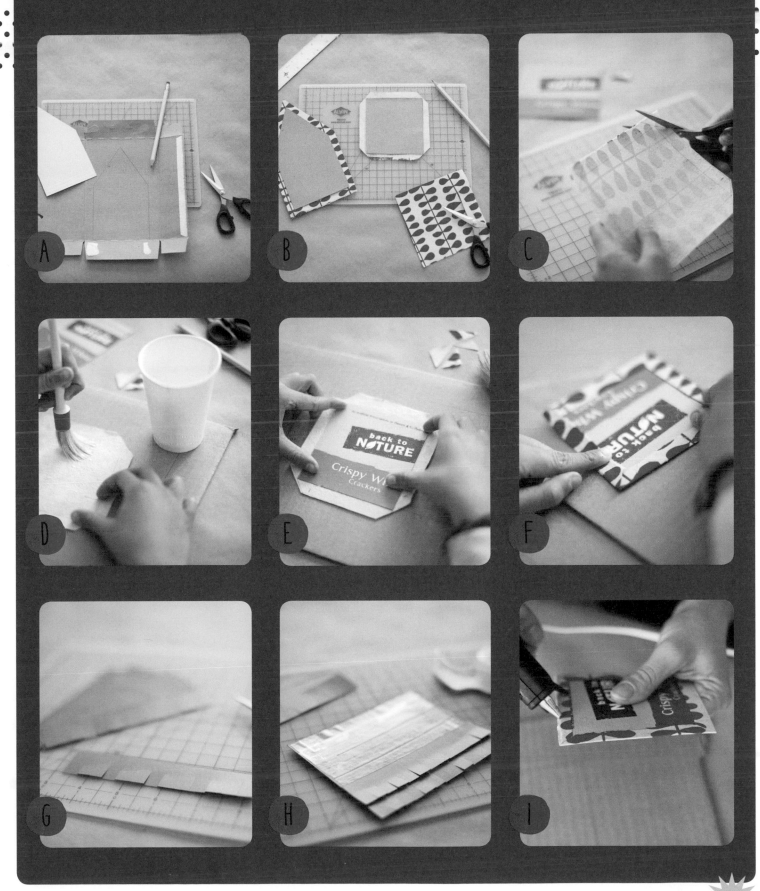

Tip: Start with the front side, because the last piece you adhere will be the most difficult and the one where glue puddles or imperfect corners are most likely to show. Remember, take deep breaths and have fun! It's only a birdhouse and it doesn't need to be constructed perfectly. You can also hide imperfections in construction with fabric trim **(fig. J)**.

10 Tape the roof panels together from underneath. Lay the decorated roof panel facedown on the table and create a space of approximately ⅛" (3 mm) between panels—this will act as your hinge and will allow the roof panels to come together without overlapping **(fig. K)**.

11 Using masking tape, adhere the two panels from the wrong side with the hinge as a ⅛" (3 mm) gap between panels. Attach string from underneath by piercing the tape and pulling the thread to the top. Reinforce the hole with additional tape if needed. Tie a square knot in the bottom of the string to keep it from pulling through **(fig. L)**.

12 Glue the roof into place with hot glue. Again, this will be easiest with two people. Be sure to hold the roof still until glue dries and sets completely. Add fabric trim to the edges **(fig. M)**.

13 To make the bird perch, cut the straw to approximately 3" (7.5 cm) and adhere to the front of the birdhouse. Add additional layers of hot glue as needed to secure—you can conceal glue with added fabric trim **(fig. N)**.

14 Continue to decorate as you wish. When finished, hang the birdhouse indoors and dream of summer days lounging in a lush garden aflutter with songbirds **(fig. O)**.

CHAPTER 4: PERFORMANCE & PUBLIC ART

TAKING ART TO THE STREETS, STAGES, AND LEMONADE STANDS

Not only do creative materials exist at every turn, so does the opportunity to push art projects into a new direction that allows for interaction and collaboration. When my son was two years old, I made him a garden gnome costume for Halloween, complete with a handmade hat, beard, and suspenders. Although he was barely old enough to grasp the concept of a holiday or annual tradition, he quickly understood that his costume allowed for a different public interaction—he could march up to our neighbors' doors and ask for candy. He could clomp around in heavy black rain boots, tip his red pointy hat, and tug at his flannel beard and be rewarded by the pleasant reactions of passing strangers.

There is something powerful about performance, costume, public art, and the impact of art outside of major art institutions. It's amazing how quickly even a toddler can understand that costumes and performance allow us to break the usual social norms. Also, art does not need to be a quiet or solitary act. The projects in this section are meant to encourage participation from family members, friends, or even the willing passersby. It's important that our children have the opportunity to see the world as their own creative space; art is not merely confined to galleries and museums—art can happen anywhere.

STYLISH SUPERHEROES: CROWNS

When my son was about eighteen months old, I made three crowns and convinced my husband to join me for a photo shoot in the nearby park for Mother's Day. I made simple crown shapes from leftover red cardstock, taped them together, and crafted accompanying star wands with straws and paper. The photos from that day's shoot are some of my absolute favorite family photographs. My toddler's crown was quickly crumbled, his wand swiftly dented, and my favorite image is of a distracted little boy standing amid the tall grasses while my husband smiles approvingly from behind. The dented crown is actually my favorite part. That activity inspired this simple crown project. Whether your little one is eighteen months or eighteen years old, we can all use a crown from time to time. If nothing else, it serves as a catalyst for a memorable photograph and playful family adventure.

MATERIALS

* decorative and/or recycled papers or two pieces of construction paper
* washi tape, optional
* scissors
* pencil
* tape
* ruler
* printing ink, optional
* brayer, optional
* soft carving blocks, optional

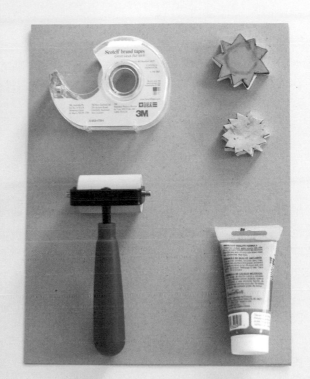

VARIATIONS

You can decorate the crown however you wish, but in the crown and wand projects I'll offer two decorative choices: using washi tape to make stripes or making simple blocks for original block printing. (You can use the same carving and printing techniques as described in the Book Page Block Printing project, page 38). You could also use stamps, crayons, colored pencils, markers, paint, or stickers to decorate your crowns.

INSTRUCTIONS

1 Measure your child's head. Remember the old adage: Measure twice, cut once. My toddler's head is 19" (48.5 cm) around and my own head is 22" (56 cm) so you'll likely want to make crowns somewhere in this realm.

2 Draw the desired shape for your crowns—you can draw a line to ensure the tops of the peaks and bases of the valleys are even or you can just go ahead and draw freehand. Cut the shapes from the paper **(fig. A)**.

3 Line two sheets of paper end-to-end widthwise. Review your shapes and how the ends of the papers will overlap. You can always alter your crown peaks slightly to make the shapes align at the seams **(fig. B)**.

4 Decorate—make stripes with the washi tape or print a simple repeat pattern with blocks. You could carve stars from carving blocks or make simple potato stamps, too. Printing, stamping, coloring, collage, and painting are all great choices. You decide! **(Fig. C.)**

5 When the paint or glue has dried completely, attach the ends of the crown with tape. If you've decorated with washi tape, you can add more tape to the mix. If you've decorated by printing or painting, you might want to fasten the two sides of the crown together from the inside with clear or matching tape. If strength is your concern, I'd suggest using clear tape to secure the edges from the exterior and interior sides of the seam **(fig. D)**.

6 Add any final embellishments—flowers, herbs, twigs, or leaves are sweet additions—and then wear with delight. No prince or princess is too old for a crown—that just makes you a king or a queen **(figs. E and F)**.

STYLISH SUPERHEROES: WANDS

These star wands are simple additions to the previous Stylish Superheroes Crown project. The crowns and wands can be made in tandem or for separate occasions. You can use the same decorative choices—block prints, washi tape, paint, collage, stamps, or even tiny found flowers or leaves. This project is simple enough for toddlers or can be embellished for older children by spending more time considering the decorations and designs. The wands make fun party favors or impromptu decorations for tea parties, too.

MATERIALS

* decorative and/or recycled papers or two pieces of construction paper
* washi tape, optional
* scissors
* pencil
* tape
* ruler
* straws or chopsticks
* printing ink, optional
* brayer, optional
* soft carving blocks, optional

VARIATIONS

Similar to the Stylish Superheroes: Crown project on page 92, you can use most any decorations to embellish your wand, but this project will focus on decorating with washi tape and printing ink.

INSTRUCTIONS

1 Fold one piece of construction paper or cardstock in half. (You could also use any found papers of similar size.) Draw a star shape and then cut through both pieces so you have a front and a back for the wand **(fig. A)**.

2 Decorate your wand using the techniques shown in the Stylish Superheroes: Crowns project on page 92 or the Performance Play: Puppet Theater on page 100. Printing, stamping, coloring, collage, or painting are all great choices. You decide! **(Figs. B and C.)**

3 Tape straw to the wrong side of one of the decorated stars. Don't worry about your tape technique—it will not show from the outside when finished **(fig. D)**.

4 Place the second decorated star on top of the taped star, sandwiching the straw in between. Tape all edges of the stars so that the wand is completely sealed on all sides. It's easiest to cut the tape lengths first and then apply the tape to the star by folding it over the edge. **(Fig. E.)**

5 Add any additional tape around the edges to make sure the straw is secured between the two stars. Make sure the two stars are taped entirely together. Now, make wishes come true by waving your wand in any magical direction—for adults and kids alike **(fig. F)**.

PERFORMANCE PLAY: PUPPET THEATER

There are so many opportunities to encourage children to embrace performance. Whether they are naturally drawn to acting on a formal stage or find their comfort zone in a home theater made of cardboard, they are likely to create stories, characters, and imaginary adventures that lend themselves to performance. The magic of live performance is not lost on the youngest child, who is likely to marvel at the sets, costumes, props, lights, and sounds that accompany dancers, actors, and musicians on stage. We can use all the design elements of a professional production to guide our home performances with little ones. The most basic set design can be achieved by using cardboard and ink to create a stage for small toys, handmade puppets, and various improvised props.

MATERIALS

* * shipping box
* * scissors
* * tape
* * ruler
* * pencil
* * ink or paint
* * brayer

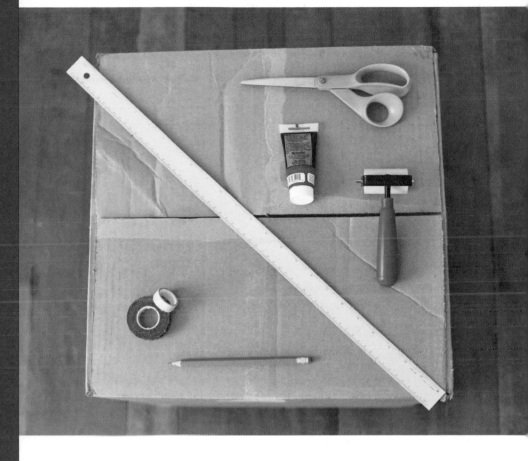

VARIATIONS

This project is decorated using tape to make stripes and red printer's ink. You could also use duct tape, markers, crayons, stamps, or wrapping paper. Consider the themes—this project uses red stripes inspired by a circus tent, but you could use red and yellow circus stripes, red and white circus stripes, black paint for a black box theater, burgundy for velvet vaudeville curtains, or purple and yellow stars for a magician's theater. Consider the child and the performance interests and let this be your design guide.

AS A PERFORMANCE MAKER, MY GREATEST JOY IS THE SENSE OF PLAY THAT HAPPENS IN EVERY GOOD REHEARSAL. MY HEART SWELLS WHEN COLLABORATORS DIVE IN WITHOUT FEAR OR HESITATION, AND THESE ARE THE MOMENTS I WANT TO CARRY INTO MY OWN LIFE. BY ENGAGING MY SON'S IMAGINATION PASSIONATELY AND REGULARLY, I HOPE HE CONTINUES TO MOVE THROUGH THE WORLD WITH ADVENTURE AND CURIOSITY.

—Erika Chong Shuch, choreographer, theater director

INSTRUCTIONS

1 Cut open the shipping box and lay it flat. Cut off all top and bottom flaps. Cut off one side so that you have three consecutive panels for the theater set. All three sides should lay open and flat. **(Fig. A.)**

2 Flip the box over to show the back side of the panels. Measure the center panel and then divide roughly by five. You'll draw one vertical line at ⅕ and one vertical line at ⅘ the total width. For example, this project measured 15" (38 cm) across the center panel, so the first vertical line was made at 3" (7.5 cm) and the second at 12" (30.5 cm)—these will be the vertical lines that create the front curtains **(fig. B)**.

3 Draw another horizontal line approximately ⅓ of the way from the top—this project measured 15" (38 cm) tall, so I made the line at 12" (30.5 cm). To make the theater curtain, draw the scallops across the horizontal line, connecting the right vertical line to the left. Cut out the drawn shape. **(Fig. C.)**

4 Flip back over to the front side of the panels. You should now have the final shape of your theater—two long sides and a front side with a curtain shape cut out. Decorate the panels as you wish. For this project, I made lines with tape and used a brayer with red printing ink to cover the entire surface. When the ink was completely dry I removed the tape to reveal the vertical stripes. **(Figs. D and E.)**

5 Decorate the interior walls if desired. Otherwise, stand the theater on a table or play surface and gather toys, make sock puppets, or create simple finger puppets to act as performers. You might even write a script, consider simple theatrical design elements such as lighting, costumes, and sound, and make infinite props with found materials. When you're ready … five minutes until curtain! **(Fig. F.)**

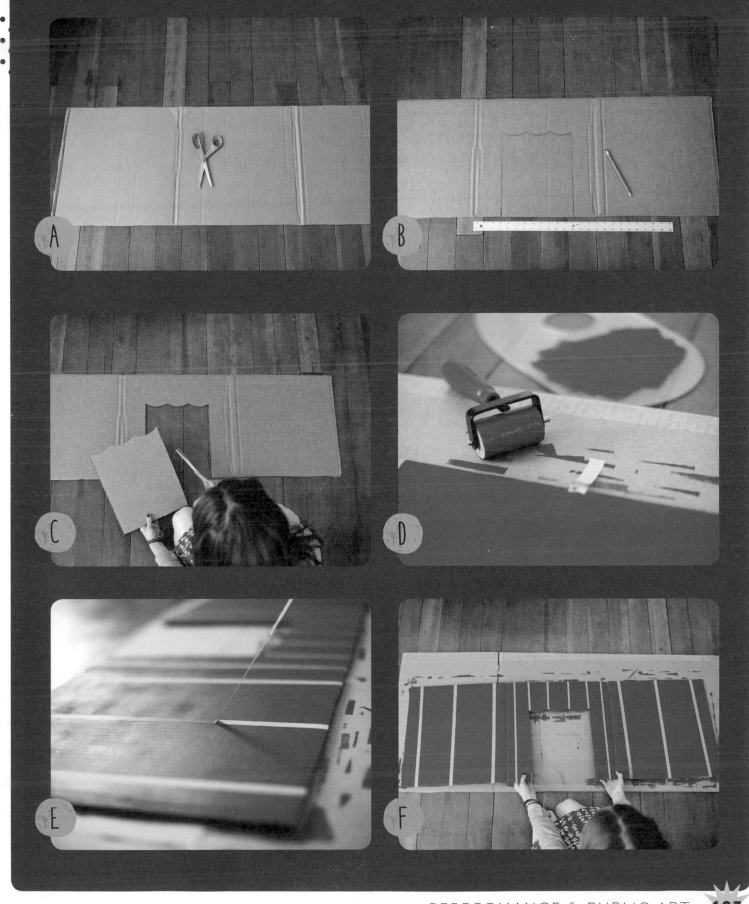

LOVE SONG ON A STRING

I love poetry. I love garlands. And I love The Beatles. So add these three loves together and the result is one love song banner on a string. Once you've made your banner you can hang it from the trees, out your front window, or string it between fence posts to declare your love to the neighborhood. You can also use it as the background for an inspired family photo shoot. The first time I made a love song banner it was Valentine's Day, and we strung our "All You Need is Love" sign in a public park as a form of public art. So peruse The Beatles' song titles for your favorite lyrics, grab some twine, and head to the streets for a photo shoot that promises to be a favorite.

MATERIALS

* standard printer paper or any paper you choose
* pencil or marker
* scissors
* paper punch
* twine
* computer and printer, optional

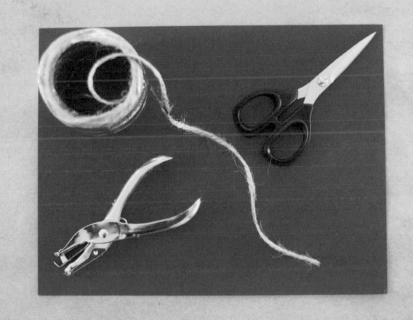

CONSIDERATIONS

Be certain to choose a song title or phrase that fits the width of your photo shoot location (Most short song titles will be long enough). For the letters in the project shown, I used standard printer paper and Franklin Gothic Medium at 760-point font. If you'd rather not use a computer and printer, you can also draw the letters by hand and cut them from the pages.

INSTRUCTIONS

1 Choose lyrics from a song by The Beatles, because they work great for love song banners. And who doesn't love The Beatles? We chose "Love Me Do" but other cute options are "All You Need is Love," "Here Comes the Sun," or "I Want to Hold Your Hand."

2 Type the title into your computer and print, or draw the letters by hand **(fig. A)**.

3 Cut letters from paper and punch two holes at the top of each letter. If your letter has two upper points, such as the letter V, punch two holes in each point for a total of four holes. **(Fig. B.)**

4 String letters on twine. Tip: Break your title in half and string the letters from each end of the twine. Leave several feet of twine at each end of the banner to provide plenty of room to tie it up **(fig. C)**.

5 Open up the banner to make certain that all letters are in place, evenly distributed, and that you have plenty of twine left at each end to tie the banner into place for the photo shoot. Having the banner already arranged will be helpful when you arrive at your photo location. If the ends of your twine are too short, simply tie on additional twine **(fig. D)**.

6 Hang between trees, fence posts, poles, etc. Set your camera on a tripod with a timer and convince your friends or family to play along! You could also convince the willing passerby to join your photo shoot for an interactive art installation. Go ahead and be silly in public—I dare you **(figs. E and F)**.

The Paper Playhouse

CLASSIC LEMONADE STAND

I grew up in a house in the country with a very long driveway that ended in the center of a tall hill. I spent my days reading in the orchard, foraging in the garden, and playing hide-n-seek in the barn, but sidewalk lemonade stands were not in my afterschool rotation. Now that I've lived in large cities, however, I regularly admire the creativity and inspiration behind neighborhood lemonade stands. This project uses shipping boxes, wrapping paper dowels, and colorful duct tape to make this unique lemonade stand that promises to garner attention from potential customers. And who knows? This clever design might just earn an extra 50 cents here and there. The original lemonade recipe will certainly be worth the extra effort—simple syrup makes everything better.

MATERIALS

* shipping box
* 2 wrapping paper tubes
* printer paper for sign
* white duct tape
* yellow duct tape
* scissors
* box cutter or utility knife, optional

CONSIDERATIONS

This project is designed to accommodate a stool, crate, or small table for the lemonade and a child's chair or second stool for seating. You could scale the project to any size table or chairs that you wish—just remember to test the height of the sign before you tape it into place, because the children should be visible underneath.

INSTRUCTIONS

1 Cut a shipping box open and lay flat. Cut off all top and bottom flaps and one side flap so you have three consecutive connected sides. Keep one extra flap for the lemonade sign **(fig. A)**.

2 Decorate three sides, two wrapping paper tubes, and one flap with alternating yellow and white duct tape to make stripes **(fig. B)**.

3 Measure the height and width of the sign and then make a smaller interior sign with printer paper—this interior sign is where you'll write, "Lemonade" with the price per glass. Have the lemonade sellers make the lemonade sign by hand—it adds extra charm. Tape your handwritten sign to the yellow and white background **(figs. C and D)**.

4 Figure out where to attach your wrapping paper tubes to the stand and measure placement. Be sure that the wrapping paper tubes are placed wide enough for your table, and leave enough room for the kids' faces to be seen from underneath the sign. Tape the base of the tubes to the inside of the lemonade stand and the top of the tubes to the lemonade sign **(fig. E)**.

5 Place the stand upright and test your stools, tables, or other furniture to make sure everything fits. Then, make lemonade! Carry lemonade stand, lemonade, cups, straws, spare change, stools, and children's chairs out to the sidewalk. Try not to drink all the lemonade yourself! Enjoy **(fig. F)**.

Lemonade Recipe
by Tracy Benjamin of Shutterbean

Makes 8 cups (1880 ml)

* 1 cup (200 g) sugar
* ½ cup (170 g) honey
* Juice from 6 lemons
* 3 cups (420 g) ice
* Lemon slices for garnish

In a large bowl, make a simple syrup by mixing the sugar and honey with 5 cups (1185 ml) boiling water. Stir until the sugar is completely dissolved. Set aside to cool. In a large pitcher, combine the lemon juice, simple syrup, 3 cups (710 ml) cold water, and stir. Adjust according to taste. If too sweet, add more water. Stir, add ice cubes and lemon slices, and then serve.

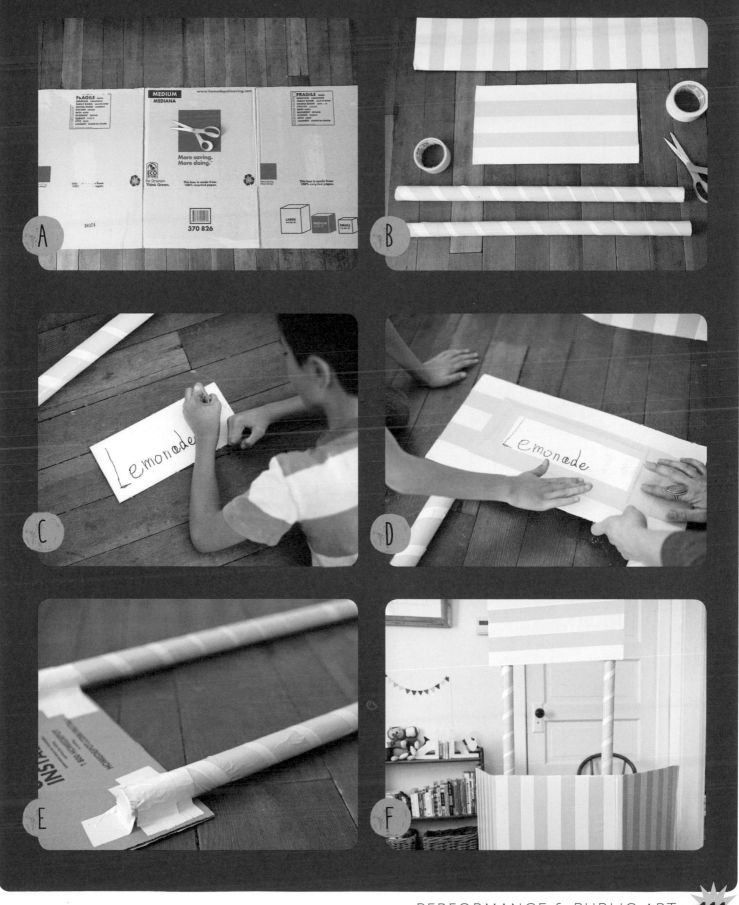

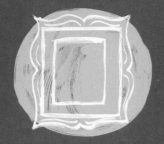

GALLERY: ARTISTS AS INSPIRATION

The artists in this gallery make work that reflects the range of projects in this book. They consider their materials in the same way you consciously or subconsciously considered your materials, thinking about texture, color, line, shape, form, value, and space. They use upcycled paper materials, paper sculpture, printmaking by hand, or otherwise alter paper to make their professional artwork. They started out just like you—experimenting with materials, learning the basics of art and design, and trusting their imaginations. Their work is varied in style, point-of-view, and intention, but their use of materials is consistent—they all use paper, books, or boxes to make art. My hope is that their work will inspire you to see the possibilities in these ordinary materials and maybe even encourage you to broaden your definition of what art can be. I hope it will inspire you to embrace the opportunities for creativity and to see the artful potential in everyday materials. More simply, I hope you will see the beauty, craftsmanship, and thoughtfulness in their work and realize this same potential resides within you.

BLACKBIRD LETTERPRESS

Blackbird Letterpress, established in 2003, is a small art printing studio in Louisiana. Specializing in stationery, paper toys, calendars, and handmade notebooks, as well as wedding ephemera, it strives for excellent craftsmanship with a small footprint.

1 Title: *Letterpress 3D DIY Tag-a-long Camper*
Year: 2012
Materials: paper, ink
Dimensions: card: 5¾" x 8¾" (14.5 cm x 22 cm), constructed camper: 3¾" x 2" x 2" (9.5 cm x 5 cm x 5 cm)

2 Title: *Letterpress 3D DIY Little Camper*
Year: 2011
Materials: paper, ink
Dimensions: card: 5¾" x 8¾" (14.5 cm x 22 cm), constructed camper: 2¾" x 1¼" x 2" (7 cm x 3 cm x 5 cm)

3 Title: *Letterpress 3D DIY Station Wagon*
Year: 2011
Materials: recycled paper, ink
Dimensions: card: 5¾" x 8¾" (14.5 cm x 22 cm), constructed wagon: 4¾" x 1½" x 1¼" (12 cm x 4 cm x 3 cm)

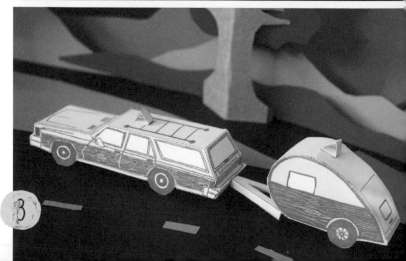

4

ESTIBALIZ HERNANDEZ DE MIGUEL

Esti is a self-taught artist, author, and illustrator, a.k.a. Pintameldia. She lives in Bilbao, Spain. She started painting in her late twenties, after a decade of involvement with the local music and art scene. All her life she's been telling stories through writing, drawing, painting, or with paper and scissors.

4 Title: *A Hundred Years of Solitude*
Year: 2012
Materials: cardstock, papercuts, glue, ink pen
Dimensions: 15" x 11" (38 cm x 28 cm)

5 Title: *Susana travels to faraway places*
Year: 2012
Materials: cardboard, papercuts, craft papers, glue, ink pen
Dimensions: 9" x 6" (23 cm x 15 cm)

5

GRACIA HABY

Besotted with paper for its foldable, concealable, revealing nature, Haby's artists' books, prints, and projects use an armory of play, humor, and poetry to lure one closer. Much of her work is included in the collections of the Australian state libraries of NSW, Queensland, Victoria; university libraries of Melbourne, Monash, RMIT; National Gallery of Australia; Print Council of Australia; Tate (UK); and UWE Bristol (UK).

1 Title: *Under the water, with a two-colour eye-glass, something similar*
Year: 2014
Materials: artists' book, unique state, featuring collage elements and pencil, with a pair of ETA Salted Peanuts Metroscopix Anaglyph 3D glasses to enable the perception of a three-dimensional scene on the printed page.
Dimensions: 10¾" x 8¾" (27 cm x 22 cm),
spread: 8¾" x 21¼" (22 cm x 54 cm)

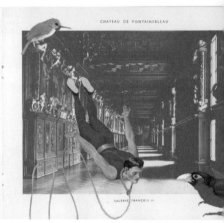

MATI ROSE MCDONOUGH

Mati Rose is a painter, illustrator, surface designer, teacher, and creative mentor. She teaches an e-course, Daring Adventures in Paint, and has illustrated several children's books, including *i carry your heart in my heart* by E.E. Cummings. She's exhibited in galleries, taught various workshops, and studied at California College of the Arts. Her book, *Daring Adventures in Paint*, was published by Quarry Books in 2012.

2 Title: *Tutti Bird*
Year: 2007
Materials: paper and fabric collage, vintage letters, paint on wood
Dimensions: 10" x 10" (25.5 cm x 25.5 cm)

3 Title: *Hollywood Beehive Betty*
Year: 2009
Materials: paper and fabric collage, vintage letters, and paint on canvas
Dimensions: 10" x 10" (25.5 cm x 25.5 cm)

4 Title: *Red Elephant*
Year: 2010
Materials: paper collage, paint, and charcoal pencil on canvas
Dimensions: 10" x 10" (25.5 cm x 25.5 cm)

KERSTIN SVENDSEN

Kerstin often finds inspiration for creative projects from memories of her childhood summers in Sweden. These images are Swedish chairs out in the sun, the table set for fika. (Fika: tea/coffee/cookie time, taken at any time of day, mostly with company and always implying coziness.) Her creative projects usually involve fabric or upcycled paper and sometimes both.

1 Title: *fika card*
Year: 2006
Materials: screenprinting ink, fabric scrap, upcycled paper
Dimensions: 4¾" x 5¼"
(12 cm x 13.5 cm)

2 Title: *fika cards*
Year: 2006
Materials: screenprinting ink, fabric scrap, upcycled paper
Dimensions: 4¾" x 5½"
(12 cm x 14 cm)

COURTNEY CERRUTI

Maker extraordinaire, Courtney is the author of *Playing with Image Transfers* and *Washi Tape*, both published by Quarry Books. Courtney is a working artist who teaches at the San Francisco Center for the Book, Makeshift Society, Press: Works on Paper,

and online at Creativebug.com. She makes something every day.

3 Title: *Feather Mobile*
Year: 2013
Materials: paper, paint, string, driftwood

4 Title: *Paper Flowers*
Year: 2012
Materials: tissue paper, wire, florist tape, found papers

JENIFER LAKE

Jenifer Lake is the owner of sprout studio—a love for pretty, handmade items joined with all things vintage. She loves to create—a knitter, a canner/jammer/pickler, a collagist, an image taker and maker, a clayer, a drawer, a painter, a jewelry maker, and a baker. Jenifer has been teaching for more than fifteen years and currently works as a visual art teacher in San Francisco.

5 Title: *untitled (lady rainbow speak)*
Year: 2010
Materials: found and collected paper ephemera
Dimensions: 4¼" x 3¾"
(11 cm x 9.5 cm)

6 Title: *untitled (bird speak)*
Year: 2010
Materials: found and collected paper ephemera
Dimensions: 4½" x 3"
(11.5 cm x 7.5 cm)

1

3

2

4

5

6

TIFFANIE TURNER

Tiffanie Turner is an architect, artist, and performer. A native East Coaster, she now lives in San Francisco with her husband and two children. Her work has been featured in numerous art blogs, the *San Francisco Chronicle*, and in her solo gallery show entitled HEADS. Tiffanie teaches classes in different paper techniques around the Bay Area under the moniker "papel SF."

1 Title: *Dahlia II*
Year: 2014
Materials: paper mâché and Italian crepe paper
Dimensions: 35" (89 cm) diameter x 14" (35.5 cm) deep

2 Title: *Peony I*
Year: 2014
Materials: paper mâché and Italian crepe paper
Dimensions: 28" (71 cm) diameter x 11" (28 cm) deep

3 Title: *Peony with Stamen I*
Year: 2014
Materials: paper mâché and Italian crepe paper
Dimensions: 23" (58.5 cm) diameter x 12" (30.5) deep

HEATHER SMITH JONES

Heather Smith Jones, MFA, is an artist working in painting, drawing, photography, and printmaking. She is an instructor at an arts-based preschool and the author of *Water Paper Paint: Exploring Creativity with Watercolor and Mixed Media*. She lives in Lawrence, Kansas, with her husband and their four felines.

4 Title: *holes in my years*
Year: 2009
Materials: graphite, watercolor, colored pencil, letterpress on paper
Dimensions: 12½" x 18" (31.5 cm x 45.5 cm)

5 Title: *I wish I knew how to turn this box into a window*
Materials: graphite, colored pencil, watercolor, letterpress on paper
Dimensions: 5" x 7" (12.5 cm x 18 cm)

6 Title: *seeds waiting to grow*
Year: 2009
Materials: graphite, watercolor, pinholes, letterpress on paper
Dimensions: 10" x 11" (25.5 cm x 28 cm)

1

2

4

OLDE

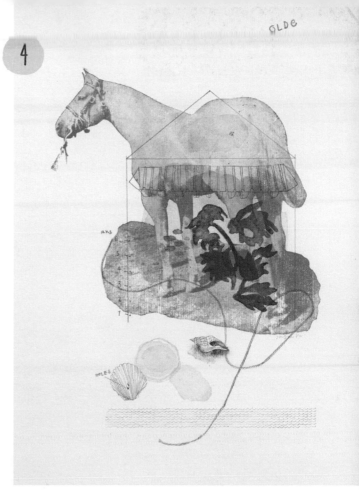

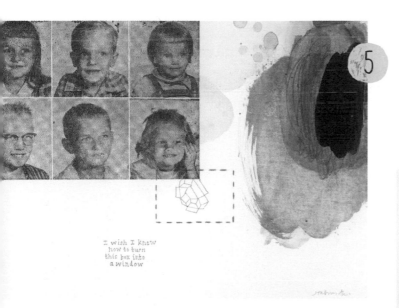

5

I wish I knew
how to turn
this box into
a window

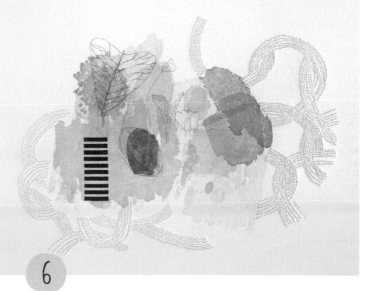

6

CORI KINDRED

Cori Kindred is a maker, thrifter, and nature-lover living in beautiful Portland, Oregon, with her partner and small son. She gathers inspiration from estate sales and vintage shops, wandering through mossy forests, and making big messes in her studio.

1 Title: *Hoyt Arboretum*
Year: 2010
Materials: vintage frame and book cover, found pinecones, seed pods
Dimensions: 11" x 14" (28 cm x 35.5 cm)

2 Title: *Fall Book*
Year: 2010
Materials: vintage book, found leaves, acorn
Dimensions: 5" x 7" (12.5 cm x 18 cm)

3 Title: *Pinecone Collection*
Year: 2010
Materials: wood box, cardboard, vintage book pages, found pinecones
Dimensions: 4½" x 6½" x 1" (11.5 cm x 16.5 cm x 2.5 cm)

MOLLIE GREENE

Mollie Greene, the artist of Royal Buffet Etsy shop, lives in Greenville, South Carolina. She has written two paper craft books: *Make & Do*, which she self-published in 2011, and *Sweet Paper Crafts*, published by Chronicle Books in 2013. Her work has been featured on numerous websites and in print.

4 Title: *Wordy Butterfly Mobile*
Year: 2009
Materials: vintage paper, metallic thread, vintage record jacket
Dimensions: 8" x 32" (20.5 cm x 81.5 cm)

5 Title: *Butterfly Gladness Garland*
Year: 2010
Materials: paper, string
Dimensions: 5" x 6' (12.5 cm x 1.8 m)

2

3

4

5

LISA CONGDON

Artist Lisa Congdon is best known for her colorful paintings and collages. She illustrates for clients including The Museum of Modern Art, *Martha Stewart Living* magazine, and The Land of Nod, among others. She is the author of *20 Ways to Draw a Tulip, Whatever You Are, Be a Good One*, and *Art Inc.*

1 Title: *Stjerner*
Year: 2011
Materials: vintage book cover, paper, shadowbox
Dimensions: 11" x 14" x 2½"
(28 cm x 35.5 cm x 6.5 cm)

2 Title: *Pine Cone*
Materials: ink on vintage book page
Dimensions: 5" x 7" (12.5 x 18 cm)

ELSA MORA

Elsa Mora is a multimedia artist born and raised in Cuba. She lives in Los Angeles. Her work has been published in books and magazines, and it has been exhibited around the world in art galleries and museums.

3 Title: *Paper Bee*
Year: 2007
Materials: acid-free paper, glue
Dimensions: 2¾" x 1½"
(7 cm x 4 cm)

4 Title: *Little Red Riding Hood*
Year: 2012
Materials: acid-free paper, glue
Dimensions: 3" x 2"
(7.5 cm x 5 cm)

JEN HEWETT

Jen Hewett is a San Francisco-based printmaker and surface designer. Her current passion is screenprinting, which she uses to create her bright, colorful work on paper and fabric.

5 Title: *Galoshes Print*
Year: 2009
Materials: screenprinting ink on paper
Dimensions: 8" x 10"
(20.5 cm x 25.5 cm)

6 Title: *Abstract Bushes*
Year: 2014
Materials: block print on paper
Dimensions: 11" x 14"
(28 cm x 35.5 cm)

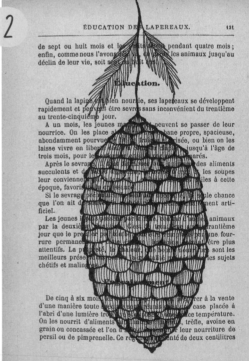

LISA SOLOMON

Lisa Solomon is a mixed media artist who moonlights as a graphic designer and professor. She often questions and deconstructs the meaning of identity and personal histories through utilizing media traditionally associated with domestic crafts. Lisa lives in Oakland, California, with her husband, young daughter, a bevy of pets, and many spools of thread.

1 Title: *2 red chairs*
Year: 2008
Materials: watercolor, acrylic, thread/embroidery on duralar
Dimensions: 8" x 8" (20.5 cm x 20.5 cm)

2 Title: *bed drawing: a green bed in green grass*
Year: 2007
Materials: watercolor, acrylic, thread/embroidery on duralar
Dimensions: 9" x 12" (23 cm x 30.5 cm)

3 Title: *we are family: yellow and brown chairs*
Year: 2010
Materials: colored pencil, thread/embroidery on duralar
Dimensions: 5½" x 5½" (14 cm x 14 cm)

4 Title: *Untitled 1*
Year: 2011
Materials: silk thread, paper
Dimensions: 24" x 18" (61 cm x 45.5 cm)
Photograph by Austin Kennedy

5 Title: *Untitled 17*
Year: 2012
Materials: silk thread, paper
Dimensions: 15¾" x 14¼" (40 cm x 36 cm)

6 Title: *Untitled Mountain 4*
Year: 2010
Materials: silk thread, paper
Dimensions: 8½" x 5½" (21.5 cm x 14 cm)
Photograph by Austin Kennedy

EMILY BARLETTA

Emily Barletta's embroidered artwork strives to record daily experiences and emotions through the simple mark making of the handmade stitch. After graduating from the Maryland Institute College of Art in 2003, she moved to Brooklyn, New York, where she currently enjoys making art at home and taking care of her plants.

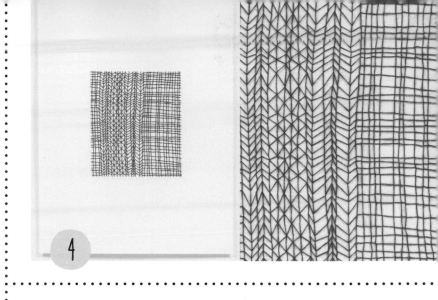

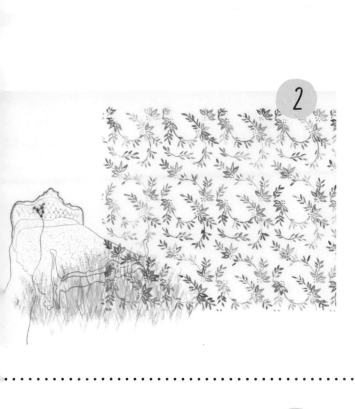

2

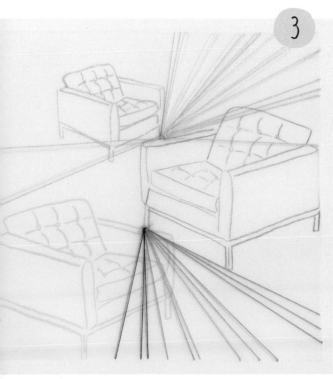

3

4

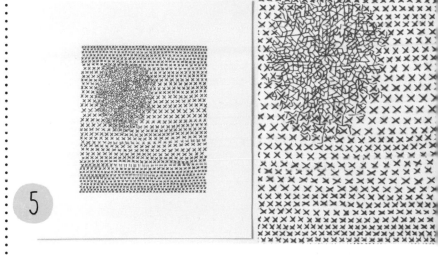

5

6

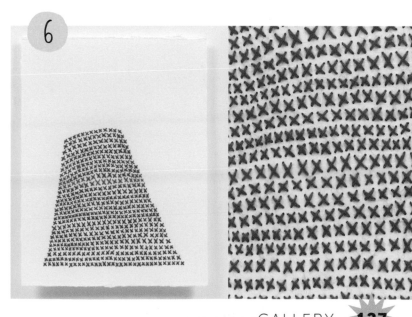

SONYA PHILIP

Sonya Philip has always made things. As a self-taught artist, she enjoys the freedom of exploring and stretching mediums. Of particular interest are all things related to textiles and fiber. Sonya lives in San Francisco with her family.

1 Title: *Ordinary Objects: Chinese Takeaway Container*
Year: 2011
Materials: box and cotton thread
Dimensions: 5" x 7"
(12.5 cm x 18 cm)

2 Title: *Ordinary Objects: Ritz Cracker Box*
Year: 2010
Materials: box and cotton thread
Dimensions: 12" x 9"
(30.5 cm x 23 cm)

3 Title: *Ordinary Objects: Reese's Pieces*
Year: 2011
Materials: cardboard and silk
Dimensions: 5½" x 3"
(14 cm x 7.5 cm)

LOUISE JENNISON WITH GRACIA HABY

Besotted with paper for its foldable, concealable, revealing nature, these artists' books, prints, and projects use an armory of play, humor, and poetry to lure one closer, and are included in the collections of the Australian state libraries of NSW, Queensland, Victoria; university libraries of Melbourne, Monash, RMIT; National Gallery of Australia; Print Council of Australia; Tate (UK); and UWE Bristol (UK).

4 Title: *As inclination directs*
Year: 2013
Materials: eight-page concertina artists' book, single-color lithographic offset print featuring collage and pencil. Printed by Redwood Prints. Edition of 10
Dimensions: 3½" x 5½"
(9 cm x 14 cm),
extended 3½" x 28¼"
(9 cm x 72 cm)

MAYA DONENFELD

Maya's distinct designs utilize sustainable resources and fibers, while weaving in elements from the natural world. Her website www.mayamade.com shares how to artfully recycle, repurpose, and reinvent. She is a frequent contributor to books and magazines and her first book, *Reinvention: Sewing with Rescued Materials*, was published by Wiley Craft in 2012.

5 Title: *paper flowers*
Year: 2010
Materials: newspaper, maps, sewing pattern paper
Dimensions: 2" (5 cm)

6 Title: *paper flowers* (details)
Year: 2010
Materials: newspaper, maps, sewing pattern paper
Dimensions: 2" (5 cm)

1

TEMPLATES

Small raindrop:
Cut 4 double-sided
or 8 total

Large raindrop:
Cut 3 double-sided
or 6 total

RAINY DAY CLOUD MOBILE
(page 20)

Raindrop Templates

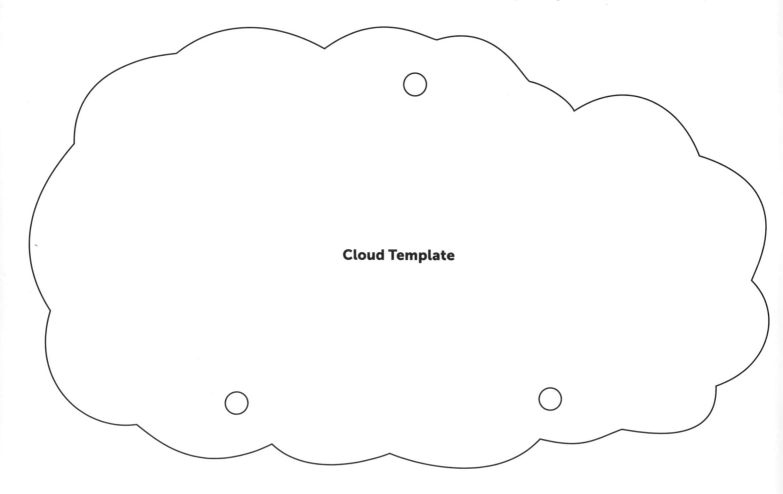

Cloud Template

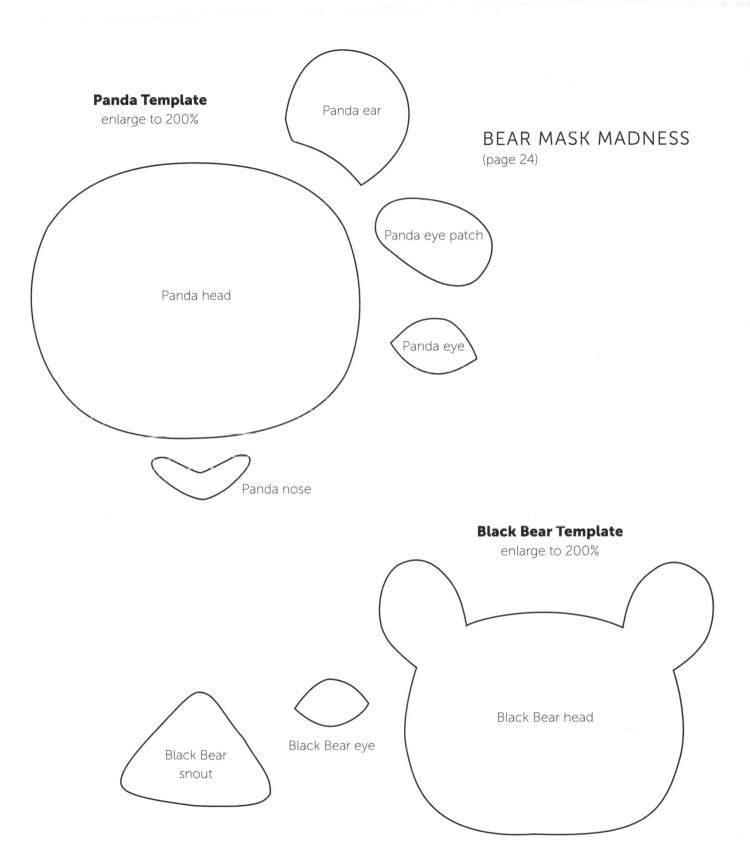

Panda Template
enlarge to 200%

Panda ear

BEAR MASK MADNESS
(page 24)

Panda eye patch

Panda head

Panda eye

Panda nose

Black Bear Template
enlarge to 200%

Black Bear head

Black Bear
snout

Black Bear eye

SCULPTURES FROM THE SEA
Sea Creature Templates
(page 28)

Bottlenose Dolphin

Sea Turtle

Blue Whale

Octopus

Starfish

Umbrella

Dress

Bag

Boots

Monster Clothing and Accessories Templates
enlarge to 200%

MOVEABLE PAPER MONSTERS
(page 32)

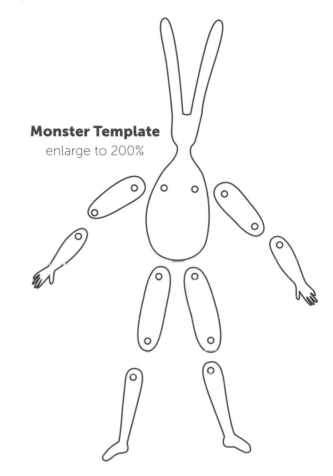

Monster Template
enlarge to 200%

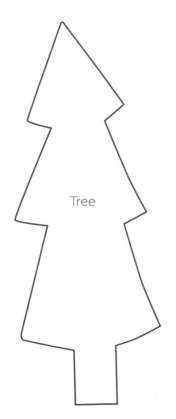

Tree

BOOK PAGE BLOCK PRINTING
Sun and Tree Templates
(page 38)

Sun

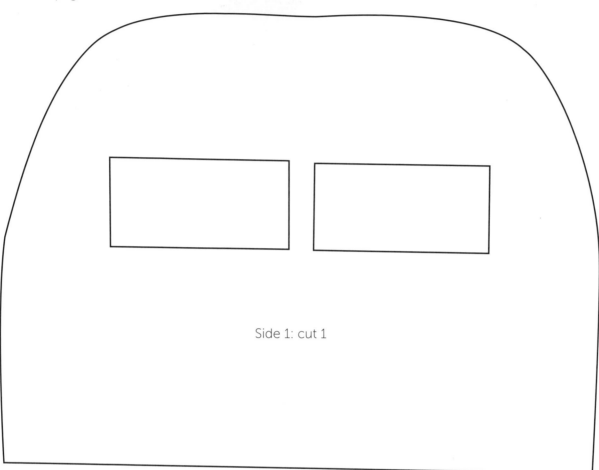

Side 1: cut 1

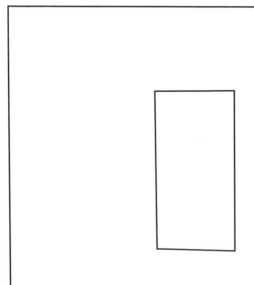

Top: cut 1

14" (35.5 cm long)

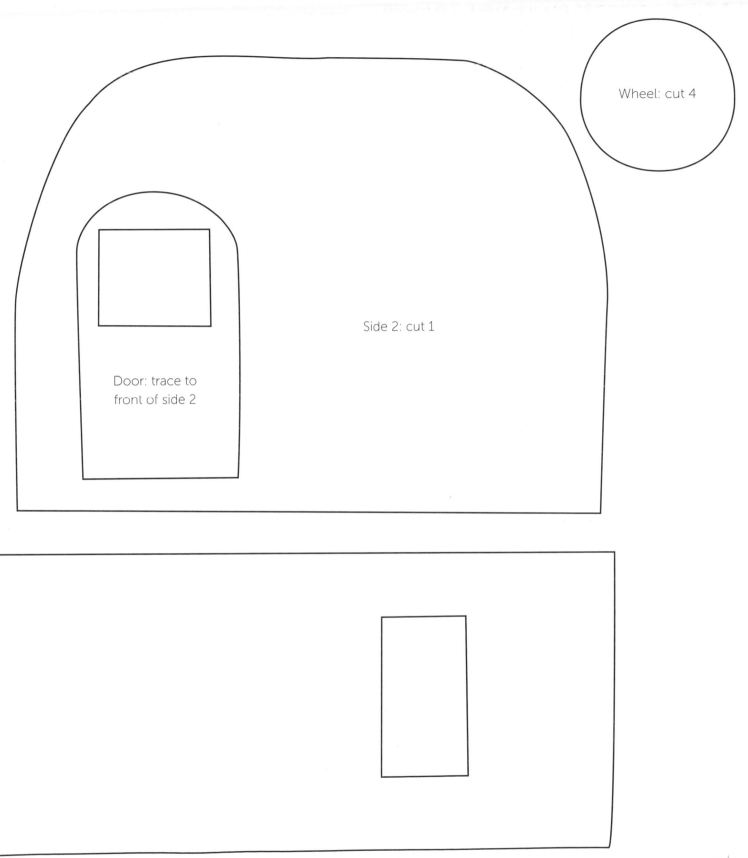

Wheel: cut 4

Side 2: cut 1

Door: trace to
front of side 2

VOLKSWAGEN BUS BOX
Side, Top, and Wheel Templates
(page 72)
enlarge to 150%

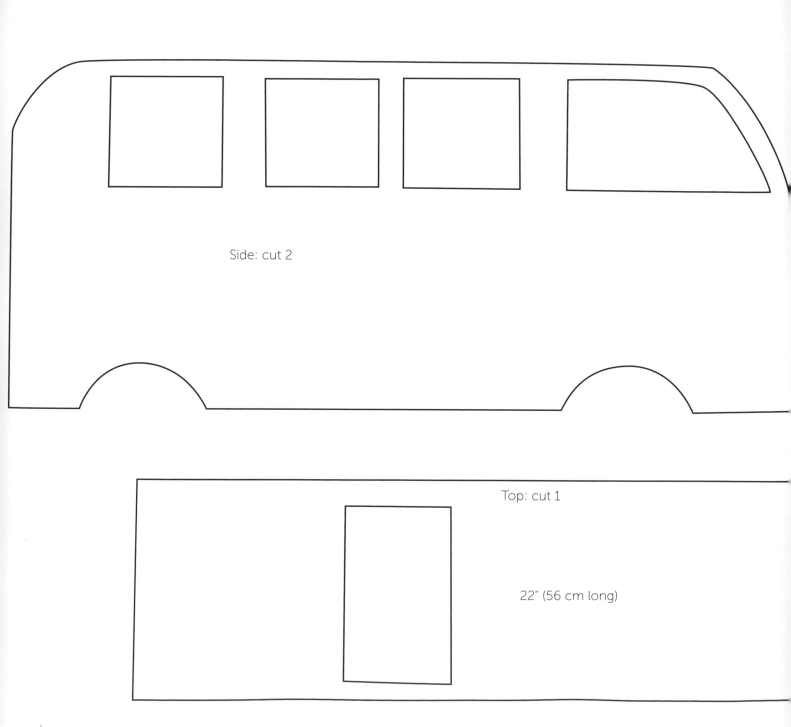

Side: cut 2

Top: cut 1

22" (56 cm long)

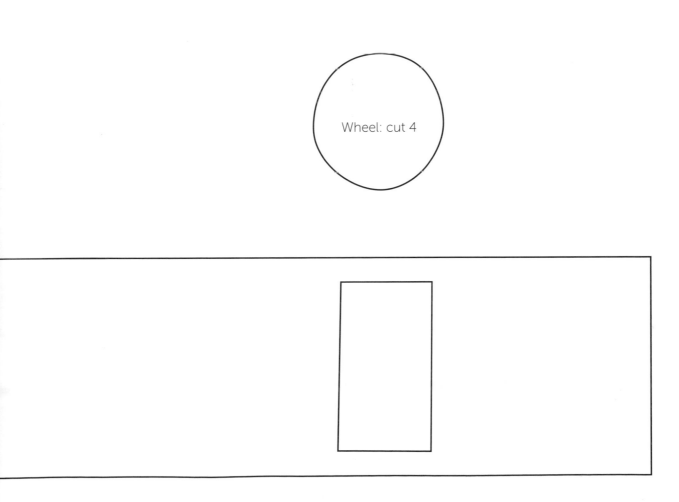

Wheel: cut 4

BIRDHOUSE BUNGALOW
Front, Back, Side, Bottom, and Top Templates
(page 84)

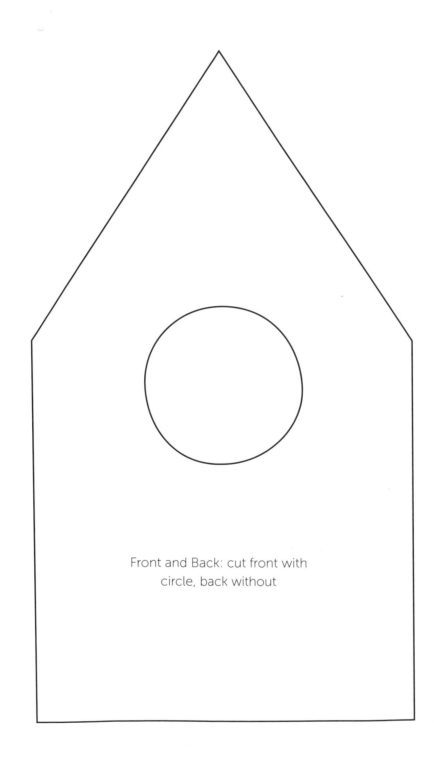

Front and Back: cut front with
circle, back without

Roof: cut 2

Sides and Bottom: cut 2 for sides
and 1 for bottom

ARTIST DIRECTORY

Ashlyn Gibson (London)
www.ashlyngibson.co.uk
www.olivelovesalfie.co.uk

Blackbird Letterpress (Baton Rouge, LA)
www.blackbirdletterpress.com

Cori Kindred (Portland, OR)
www.corikindred.com

Courtney Cerruti (Hayward, CA)
www.ccerruti.com

Elsa Mora (Los Angeles)
www.allaboutpapercutting.com

Emily Barletta (Brooklyn, NY)
www.emilybarletta.com

Erika Chong Shuch (Berkeley, CA)
www.erikachongshuch.org

Estibaliz Hernandez de Miguel (Bilbao, Spain)
www.pintameldia.com

Gracia Haby (Victoria, Australia)
www.gracialouise.com

Heather Smith Jones (Lawrence, KS)
www.heathersmithjones.com

Jen Hewett (San Francisco)
www.jenhewett.com

Jenifer Lake (San Francisco)
www.sproutstudio.net

Jessica Smith (Birmingham, AL)
www.looktouch.wordpress.com

Kerstin Svendsen (Alameda, CA)
www.shashtin.com

Lisa Congdon (Oakland, CA)
www.lisacongdon.com

Lisa Solomon (Oakland, CA)
www.lisasolomon.com

Louise Jennison (Victoria, Australia)
www.gracialouise.com

Mati Rose McDonough (Oakland, CA)
www.matirose.com

Maya Donenfeld (Trumansburg, NY)
www.mayamade.blogspot.com

Mollie Greene (Greenville, SC)
www.molliegreene.com

Samantha Giles (Oakland, CA)
www.smallpresstraffic.org

Sonya Philip (San Francisco)
www.sonyaphilip.com

Tiffanie Turner (San Francisco)
www.papelsf.com

Tracy Benjamin (San Rafael, CA)
www.shutterbean.com

ACKNOWLEDGMENTS

I would like to thank my amazing editor, Mary Ann Hall, for her continued support, encouragement, and unwavering vision for this book. I am so grateful for this opportunity. I'd also like to thank Heather Godin, Cara Connors, and the entire team at Quarry Books—thank you for every detail and insight. Thank you to my amazing photographer and talented friend, Leslie Sophia Lindell. I am so grateful for your artistry, humor, and companionship all the way through this process. Thank you to my dear parent friends who allowed their children to appear in these pages! Karisa, Kathryn, Sonya, Jennifer, Melissa, Pascale, and Pati—thank you so much. And to the children in this book—you are the ultimate inspiration—Maxwell, Roscoe, Luca, Celeste, Beatrice, Taeo, Phoenix, Benjamin, Rowan, Noemi, Daniela, Hugo, Marely, Aden, and Mona. Thank you to all the artists who contributed work to the artist gallery—I am humbled and honored to share these pages with you and your inspiring work. Thank you to Suzanne at Interface Art Gallery for sharing her beautiful space. Thank you to Mati Rose for insisting this book was possible.

Thank you to my amazing San Francisco Bay Area arts community—you inspire me beyond measure. Thank you to all the artists, writers, designers, thinkers, dreamers, and readers I've met online or through my blog—I am forever grateful for your encouragement and firmly believe this book exists because of you. Thank you to my amazing family (all of you) and specifically to my beloved mother for teaching me how to sew, use a glue gun, and identify treasures. Thank you to my best friend, Shauna Casey, for being my ultimate cheerleader in all adventures since first grade. And, last, to my loving husband, David Szlasa, thank you for 1,000 things every day of every week of every year that we've been making our art dreams come true.

ABOUT THE AUTHOR ·:·:·:·:·

Katrina Rodabaugh is an artist, writer, and crafter working primarily with paper, textiles, and natural objects. She earned her BA in environmental studies from Ithaca College in New York and her MFA in creative writing/ poetry from Mills College in California where she trained and taught in the Book Art Studio. She's committed to using recycled, found, and/or biodegradable materials to maintain an environmentally friendly art studio. Her work is interdisciplinary, embraces traditional women's craft techniques, and often explores sustainability, domesticity, or communication. Her artwork, writing, and designs have been shown in numerous galleries, special collections, journals, and theaters across the country, and her handmade crafts have appeared in online shops and juried craft fairs. She was a writer-in-residence at the Vermont Studio Center and has been awarded artist grants from The Puffin Foundation, The Zellerbach Family Foundation, and the Creative Capacity Fund. Her blog, *Made by Katrina*, won the *Country Living* Blue Ribbon Blogger Award. She's originally from upstate New York, but currently lives in Oakland, California, with her husband, young son, and tiny urban garden. Visit www.katrinarodabaugh.com